A MIND BLOWN IS A MIND SHOWN

Copyright © 2024 Steve Krakow

Published Exclusively and Globally by Far West Press

All rights reserved. No part of this book may be reproduced in any form or by any electronic or mechanical means, including information storage and retrieval systems, without written permission from the publisher or author, except in the case of a reviewer, who may quote brief passages in a review. Scanning, uploading, and electronic distribution of this book or the facilitation of such without the permission of the publisher is prohibited. Your support of the author's rights is appreciated.

www.farwestpress.com

First Edition

ISBN 979-8-9887354-6-5

Printed in the United States of America

Thank you...
SEG, Mom/Pop/Fam, Taralie, KA, Georgia, Tracy, Nathan, Makoto, Hiroshi, Tabata, Tsuyama, Lawrence, Lux, Lush, Matt S, Andrew P, Erica V, Hideout, E Bottle, Chicago Reader/P Montoro/A True, Yonkers, Annette, Ono, Flashlight, Jake A, Simon F, Scott W, Frankie D, James P, D City, Rocco, Terry R, Ed A, Clint S, Arthur B, Marx Bros, Monty P, K Wahl, Lester B, Grant M, Libs, BBB, Suzy P, Tristian/Juliet, M and R Fry, Godsy, Jose/Dru/Rob

RIP..
Joe C, Cat Chow, Tony C, Michael C, Damo S, Michael K, Jutok K, Phil C, Daevid A, Clive P, Simeon, Nik T, John R and Bert/Loren J

My P's dressed me pretty dang well at age 2

Arbitrary Illumination

I'm just going to come out and say that reading the opening "childhood years" of any memoir-ish volume is the toughest slog for this biography-addict. I'll admit a few have been straight-up skipped as I've headed straight for the juicy/relevant stuff. So feel free to jump ahead if you like, but having basically learned how to read from comic books, it seems crucial to have an origin story. I do wish I could say I was rocketed or beamed down from a dying planet, but as my immediate midwestern self-deprecation here might indicate, I was in fact born at Edgewater Hospital in Chicago on 9/30/73 (now torn down, it was looking like a cool abandoned horror movie set for years though).

My folks grew up in the city, the Krakow side of the fam had been in Chicago for a while by the time my dad Ira M was born in 1947. The clan had even made a mark on the Windy City as fish peddlers, with both a shop in Rogers Park (where my P's met), and a stand on the famed immigrant market Maxwell Street. Also helping out with the fishes was my great uncle, Harry "King Levinsky" Krakow, who was a semi-famous boxer (Ira Berkow's famous book, *Maxwell Street: Survival in a Bazaar*, talks about Levinsky and the fam fish stand). My pop was too busy slinging sea creatures to pay attention to the later-deified blues musicians that would perform regularly at the marketplace in that 60s period, and of course I drool reading about Papa Charlie Jackson and Robert Nighthawk playing. Levinsky/Harry K would also peddle ties, and lore has it he tried to pull his usual salesman scam on one Al Capone (the old "two ties for $10, one for $5 but oh I have no change, so you get two" bit) and Capone loved his "moxie." I was always led to believe Levinsky wasn't the sharpest bulb (he was known for murdering the Engish language) and not even a great fighter, but he had a pretty solid record, beating an aging Jack Dempsey and kinda infamously lasting in the ring about 30 seconds with Joe Louis. Levinsky also opened a bar downtown and a giant brawl destroyed it within days, and he married not one, but two "fan dancers." His sister and manager, Leapin' Lena, who also helped out at the fish market, and was known for a foul mouth and temper.

My mother Sandra was a second-generation immigrant and her mother Hilda, from Będzin, Poland came to the USA in 1922. Without going into too much straight-ahead history, or veering into total darkness for a book beginning (though ok, get ready for childhood murder traumas), the southern city had a vibrant Jewish community until the Nazis rolled in 1939, soon with death squads in tow. The city was ghetto-ized in 1942, and a year later most of the populace was sent to Auschwitz. But a few of my relatives are rumored to have escaped, and fled to Switzerland, South America, and other corners of the world. Growing up with this devastating knowledge could not help but shape this lad, at least making me aware of true evil (outside of comics) existing, and yes, the complication/prejudices of growing up a Jew. I did not grow up with many fellow members of the tribe, a childhood neighbor had never even heard of or seen a bagel before (heresy). In school, pre-conservative whitewashing I guess, doing a book report in junior high I learned that thee USA was possibly not to be trusted, complicit in sending back boatloads of Jews back to Poland to be killed. I also learned a great uncle did not make it out and died in the camps, as the rest of the family fled and first headed to Ellis Island, then Chicago, with some seven siblings in a one bedroom apartment. My grandfather Hyman worked at the Illinois Molding picture frame company on Western Ave, coincidentally a street I'd eventually live on for some 27 years.

I guess i had a fairly "normal" upbringing northwest of Chicago, in an area which a friend once described as "the most suburb-y suburbs ever," and they're not wrong. It was different in the daze before the strip malls and utter monoculture moved in, and this introspective/shy-but-not/blabbermouth of a kid could still find solace in the past, as I gravitated to the Chicago oldies music station that my parents played. Legendary local and rebellious 60s DJ Dick Biondi (RIP) would often still host, and introduce me to artists like Love and Link Wray, via his "from the vaults" deeper cut asides—he brushed past me once at a Del Shannon concert in a bank parking lot, and I was starstruck (Del walked past me too, a guy I always loved and still do, his sad psych LP and otherwise). As a kiddo, I'd also see some versions of the Drifters, Beach Boys, and the Box Tops (perhaps with a struggling Alex Chilton, as he'd often do those reunions in the 80s, but I don't remember). I also inherited my parents' records of the Byrds, Simon and Garfunkel, etc and mom's portable/fold up suitcase record player (the speakers unhinged and came off, which I thought was cool). According to mum, I was drawing by age 3, which I think most kids do, they just aren't encouraged/interested and often stop. I'd often sketch my childhood pup, Flashlight, but copying stuff out of comics was more or less my "training." I also loved book illustrators like Mercer Meyer, Maurice Sendak, and Richard Scarry from about day one. Another big influence was local kid's TV host Bill Jackson, who would draw a full comic strip in real time, and sculpt into a clay creature called "Blob", adding hand-drawn features. There was plenty of great programming at night of Twilight Zone and old horror movies, that I watched on a black and white TV, to the dismay of my lil' 80s friends. I took a few drawing classes at the local park district with a few kind teachers I looked up to (shout to Kevin Wahl wherever ya are), and I'm grateful as it was what we could afford on my dad's dual jobs as a weekend wedding photographer and testing coffee grounds in a lab. My mom was always a younger-ages teacher, but she gave it up for a while to raise us, as somehow a family could afford this "American Dream" in the late 70s-early 80s.

We could visit free art events (like the yearly Gold Coast Art Fair) and the Art Institute and other museums often. Cheap shopping at flea markets and garage sales was an education in itself, as I'd randomly pick up classic rock LPs I'd heard of, from Sabbath to Yes, often based on cool cover artwork. I'd also grab paperbacks, monster mags, comics, posters, other plentiful memorabilia that was not so "collectible" yet—though by age 12 i was going to proper comic conventions in old suburban veteran halls and hotels. It kinda blows my mind now that I could just walk up to the creator of Mad Magazine (and in many ways classic Jewish humor) Harvey Kurtzman, or

Mad's "fastest artist" Sergio Aragones and ask for free sketches. If ONLY I'd met my fave, "Mad's Maddest Artist" Don Martin, who I drew in the style of from 2nd-3rd grade for my first linear comic project—a Welcome Back Kotter "fan fiction" story in pencil (how little things have changed). I also met a lot of heavy comic book idols like Stan Lee, op art innovator Jim Steranko, classic Superman artists Curt Swan and Kurt Schaffenberger, Swamp Thing co-creator Bernie Wrightson, Rocketeer creator Dave Stevens (RIP), and tons more--who yeah, would also do lil' sketches if you asked. Today these extravaganzas are like $100 an autograph with long queues and tons of "cosplay." To sound like a geezer, boy, was comic collecting "not cool" in the 80s, it had a coded language only male true geeks seemingly understood, as literally zero females were present (and most superhero comics were so sexist, this made sense). For me, comics (and especially their artwork) were still a suburban escape like none other, as I discovered the futurist/ cosmic worlds of old gods like Kirby, Ditko/Colan's Dr. Strange, Silver Surfer, etc--oddly the same stuff the heads of the 60s came up on, escaping their grey childhoods. Riding my bike to get the fresh comics every week was a ritualistically joyous time, and at my local shop (part of the small Moondog's chain) one of the staffers would draw his pro-ish comics while working, definitely a future inspiration (boy, did I try drawing at every job I ever had, though not at my first shit jobs, when I lied about my age to become a janitor and bag-boy). There was also a Rose Records (another small chain) in the same decaying shopping center, where I'd start to peek into the cut out bins and I could buy concert tix there in the future (yup, only at certain "outlets" in those dayz).

As i eluded to earlier, some infamy lurked under this veneer of this suburban normalcy. My fam first lived in a townhouse on the Mt. Prospect/Des Plaines border, very close to when and where John Wayne Gacy operated, but we moved when my brother Adam was born in 1977. The under-developed Hoffman Estates (where there was truly no estates, just cornfields and dirt) is where I truly grew up. These were the days of parents never quite knowing where their un-cell-tracked kids were, until we came back at dinner time. So we roamed/biked the plains freely, feeding horses in nearby stables, catching bugs, and scaling the few dirt mounds in the area. My neighborhood friends appeared in my grade school VHS-recorded movies that I'd "direct," via my dad's not-sure-how-we-afforded-it tech obsession. Ask anyone who has seen it, my first film, The Piano, is an inadvertent comedy classic, and my version of Dracula is pretty er, well, its about 5 minutes long. I still day-dreamed of having true adventures like those I saw in period-adolescent movies like the Goonies, Time Bandits, or the pretty-dark-n'-angsty Stand By Me (god, I wished i could go on a quest to find a dead pirate/body with my friends). Speaking of this morbidity, one might think growing up in a family-populated cul de sac in suburbia would be a pretty benign existence, but it was not. Serious alcoholism and abuse was prevalent in a lot of households, which I'd catch glimpses of, and we'd find out later that things were very dark indeed with the family at the end of the modest court we lived on—as my childhood pal ended up being a convicted mass murder.

The Degorskis figured heavily in my youth, I

kinda had a crush on the eldest sister, who was a bit like cousin Marilyn on the Munsters, she stood out as very normal and studious, whereas the rest of the family were a bit like suburban hillbillies the Klopeks (in the immortal film the 'Burbs, natch). I'd come over to tape her Kool and the Gang and Police 45s, and stay to play with her younger brothers' legos (we had the inferior Loc Blocs) and Odyssey (pre-Atari 2600 home video game system, which was a step above "pong"). The eldest brother James aka Jim, was a year older than me, and would come to my childhood birthday parties of like bowling and going to see Mad Max Beyond Thunderdome at the cheap theatres. We moved to the other thrilling side of Hoffman Estates in 1988, and five years later a massacre of seven people took place in a local Brown's Chicken chain restaurant in nearby Palatine. It went unsolved for a decade, due to bungling of the evidence by out-of-their-league suburban cops. I'll let you morbid "true crime heads" look up most of the truly chilling details, but in a brief nutshell, Jim met his partner Juan De Luna in high school, who had a grudge against his former fast food employer. I'd heard Degorski had already been in trouble with the traditional juvenile delinquency stuff of boosting cars, busted with weed, etc but little prepared me for the news that they were arrested for this veritable "thrill killing" (tough Jim maintains his innocence on his prison website). I was visiting New York at the time when I got the news, and just wandered around in a daze that day, thinking about how one can get to that murderous point, and the more ominous side of human of nature. Growing up with Jim, it hit me again how most young boys are fascinated with death and power, monsters, violence etc. My pal Frankie, who was a bad kid but did not go there, said once, "At the library we went right for the books with pictures of dead bodies"—and I remember doing the same. In some status-symbol-land isolation, with abuse at the hands of a deranged father (who brought a loaded gun to work once, a lot less common in those days), these demons can clearly go unchecked--it's no secret a lot of serial killers are midwestern, suburban types. Even more mind-boggling, in the friggin' cul de sac next to mine (where both my math and gym teacher lived), murder would rear its head in another home I played in as a child. The homeowner in 1991 was a pilot, Mark Wilkinson, who killed his wife and started dismembering the body in the garage, before fleeing in a plane and being forced down by authorities. Needless to say this also made major news at the time.

As stated, we moved to another side of town before a lot this infamy started, but this also caused me to go to a different high school right off the bat, casting me as a pretty instant outcast even more than I would've been, in those years of angsty struggle (think more geek than freak though). Upon entering HS, I knew not a soul, and naturally everyone else had been long term buddies, and I left mine behind. Add in not being good at sports, ladies being a total mystery, growing pains, and it was not the best of times, like for most teenagers. As "the kid who could draw" I DID avoid beatings, I could sketch up Eddie from the Iron Maiden covers for thee heshers, and superhero crud impressed the jocks enough to leave me be. I pretty-nerdily worked on the yearbook and became graphics editor at the school newspaper, where I would also be indulged to write articles. Yeah, I had writer aspirations too, i excelled in poetry classes I'll admit, really because of deep dives into ol' Jimmy Morrison. I know peeps hate da bastid, but the Doors led me to the Velvet Underground, not to mention the typical fatalist/wasted/illuminated poets ala Rimbaud, Thomas, and Blake. By the end of high school I was seeking out more west coast 60s bands besides the Doors, via Nuggets LP and cassette comps from a surprisingly great local library (which had like Buckley n' Beefheart)... and I finally kinda "rebelled" in tandem with this more radical music. After hearing a teacher was having relations with the students, I took part in my first underground newspaper and nearly got expelled. Said teacher threatened to sue, but a fellow conspirator had a parent who was a high-powered attorney, and I don't think he wanted the facts to come out (he had literally bragged to the kids he coached)...it was dropped. I was also saved by some nom de plumes being used, an early lesson-- despite my cartooning being recognized. My P's were so not thrilled, and I could not take part in my graduation ceremony (oh, the pain), but girls I hardly knew were calling me, I was suddenly being hailed as a hero (at graduation incognito it was high fives galore) and I saw the "power of the underground press"!

Art skool exhibition of various groovy installations using found objects/readymades

Th' year(s) punk broke, I think

In high skool, I'd also grab the ubiquitous Morrison biography, *No One Here Gets Out Alive*, reading about "hearing colors and seeing sound," so I was itching to get out of my parents' house and get onto that world-- maybe even somehow playing music myself, as promised piano lessons never materialized, and I was not encouraged to play music in school. Art classes were probably enough I guess, but I remember being bummed that an old guitar of my uncle's at my family home vanished one day. At school, in downstate Illinois, at the University of Illinois in Urbana-Champaign, I jumped into then-current albums like Primal Scream's *Screamadelica* and My Bloody Valentine's *Loveless*, which sorta confirmed that audio hallucinations could be real, and music became infused into my DNA in a new but familiar way---it was never light entertainment to me, but some intangible magic trapped in the air for but a second, that could effect one as deeply as anything that enters the body. Some say life is a but a vibration, as our cells and all matter does, but these sonic waves could induce trance states, trigger memories in Alzheimer's patients, and well, transform souls in the right circumstances.

It was also a pretty dang golden time for indie aka truly independent/DIY music, but I sure did not know it back then. 1991-95 aka my university years, were perhaps the heyday of "college/alternative rock" or any other meaningless term you wanna come up with. The school's classic rock station literally changed to "alt rock" my sophomore year, and had no idea what to play besides breakout "buzz" bands, so you'd hear noisy stuff like Sonic Youth and Dinosaur Jr in place of the former Steve Miller Band and Blues Bros soundtrack (though I have no problem with either).

Via Champaign record shops like Record Swap, Record Service, and the local indie distro Parasol (thanks for letting me in the warehouse, boys) it was pretty easy to dig a little deeper to discover lo-fi New Zealand stuff like the Clean and Tall Dwarfs, bedroom pop from the old Elephant 6 tapes/45s to Flying Saucer Attack, heady shoegaze imports like Teenage Filmstars to Sweet Jesus, and scuzzy grunge. Yes, Grunge (TM) especially ruled Chambana (as the dual cities were often known) ala local heroes like Hum and Poster Children, who were both courted by major labels as the "next Nirvana." C-U was firmly on "the indie circuit" then, so seeing touring bands like Bailter Space, Math from Chicago (who were probably the first "experimental band" I ever saw), Mazzy Star, Unrest (who blew my mind playing one chord for 15 minutes once), Wedding Present (make no mistake, they could out Velvets-fuzz n' jangle them all), Royal Trux, and Shudder to Think (who knew this was emo? if so, I liked it then). I would also head 2-3 hours to Chicago to see grungers like Mudhoney a zillion times (always a giant pit) to yes, Nirvana (the only time they ever played "You Know You're Right") ; and shoegaze bands galore like MBV (lost a toenail at one show), Swervedriver, Verve, Ride, Medicine, Lush, etc. I even hit raves, as it was the era (a Psychic TV one with old Genesis P-Orridge was particularly fun).

All this show action more or less confirmed that

MAYBE I could play guitar if I had a battery of effects pedals, one power chord, and a few ideas. I got my first guitar at a thrift (a broken Conrad) that someone literally screwed a heavy metal rod onto so i could "whammy", but staying in tune was not an option. Luckily a roomie who was in local shoegaze band Drown, gave me a cast-off metal ax, a Peavey Predator, plus a flange and shitty distortion pedal to use, and I was off and running/badly strumming. I started immediately recording my own lame little faux-VU riffs and tunes on a handheld tape recorder. My first "public sound performance" was on the "sidestage" at yearly C-U institution Band Jam (where the Poster Kids and the like played, also grunge-adjacent stuff like Hardvark, 16 Tons, Steakdaddy Six, and the much underrated Love Cup), playing a drone on a keyboard as said guitar roomie played an acoustic MBV cover. My "musical partner" was outraged that I'd wear a bright green cardigan onstage is about all I can remember, and that no one could tell I was playing an instrument, they thought I might just be sitting there. I also played at the decaying painting studios (yeah, somehow majoring in illustration was not an option) at an art opening. I played pure noise as part of the duo Moleculad, which I had with another roomie, the very-talented actual painter/musician Nathan Rosser, with my industrial pal Greg sitting in (who turned me onto Can, Coil and Throbbing G, bless 'im). The ramshackle art department left us alone to do weird stuff and my first "happenings" out at "the studios," which were merely sectioned off areas in the rundown, former Forestry Science building. Football, the horrific Greek system, and the gleaming, modern engineering campus really took priority at the Big Ten school, but it led to a true underground scene away from all that, maybe JUST before cultural rebellion had been completely bought and packaged (I remember said frathouses cranking Fugazi and Smashing Pumpkins by the end of my tenure). My teachers were mostly stodgy, frustrated formalists who could not make it as actual working artists, so I found myself playing the part of "art skool rebel" for the zillionth generation. I was inspired by the Dadaists and their readymades, impermanent installations, and subverting the "grand history" and canon of art. I happily made an instructor cry when I literally wiped my butt with a canvas for the lame assignment of "use a new medium" (did he touch it? I won't reveal). Luckily a few cool TA's sort of took me under their wing, Native American artist Olen Perkins just about saved my life, as he hated the school's racist "chief" mascot (a white guy in "Indianface"), tuned me into Roky Erickson and other amazing music, took me to cool art exhibitions, and he gave me the dirt on my other professors (one who plagued me with endless still life drawings was a bad junkie). Only later did I find out the school had been an avant garde music center, with John Cage in residence in the 60s, leading to groundbreaking electronic bands like Spoils of War.

Senior year, I joined the band playing in my slum of a house basement (one could literally see through a hole on the second floor into the first). The band was already going before I joined, as all hailed from nearby Decatur, and they could never quite come up with a name, but Palmolive was bandied about in tribute to the Raincoats/Slits drummer (but the name was taken). I fashioned myself to be on "helicopter noises" on guitar, and never could quite add to their Throwing Muses cover, but I tried. Rosser was on drums; Taralie Peterson aka Tar Pet, Louise Bock, and Tekla Peterson was on guitar and vocals; and Kathleen Baird aka Traveling Bell and KA Baird, was on bass/vocals. The latter two would later start amazing bands Scumkid and the longstanding avant-folksters Spires That in the Sunset Rise. This nameless outfit played one successful show in our basement at a party, and then an utter disaster at a house show across town. The single crappy amp that had both Peterson's and my guitar foolishly coming out of it, blew up almost immediately. Taralie threw her guitar into the crowd, with stunned onlookers dodging it, and she fell to her knees sobbing. The bass and drums carried on, and my painting studio bud Chet Grenda hopped on vocals, but it all petered out quickly, end of the band. The aforementioned Scumkid who followed (with Georgia Vallas) were much better anyhow, a truly intuitively messed-up band that sounded like Teenage Jesus and the Jerks falling down the stairs with the Birthday Party, for incredibly epic 6+ minute songs. Recording their early shows on my brother's 4-track and releasing some of their demented tunes on a CDR (with block-printed packaging) was one of my earliest attempts at a DIY music release (Check out the film they made in the day online too, it's truly mad).

Not having a particularly difficult major but access to school resources indeed led me to doing more zines, in a reversal of sorts, the means justified the end. (I even made apocalyptic super 8 films because they had the facilities, that shit was expensive!) I had a hook-up in the school printing department, so i created a "superhero head comic" (heavy on the groovy Doctors Strange and Fate), which in retrospect, was sort of my transition between "the future" and my youth of wanting to draw straight-up mainstream comics (as i also taught myself the basics of lettering, panel borders, inking etc as a lad). This was simply called Psychedelic Comics, and I learned getting those suckers assembled was no easy task, as even finding a longarm stapler was tough (I would often lay the mag open/flat onto a board, staple, pull it out, then fold the staples over, not great on your hands). My next periodical was "Blissed-Out Funnies", an eclectic, VERY Last Gasp/Rip-Off Press-style underground comic, once again done ala free xerox machine access and very organically. I'd redevelop some of this latter zine's material into Third Eye Comics, which I sent to indie publishers and got nada. Some of its contents would also become cannibalized for my first *Galactic Zoo Dossier* magazine.

Galactic Anglodelica

To backtrack a touch, I'm convinced the very flat cornfield-ness of the Midwest encouraged me to hallucinate mountains out of the clouds hovering above the plains. So, I was always drawn to myths taking place in canyons, hills and seas, fighting magical beasts and evil gods. Hence, I gravitated towards very UK-centric culture like Roger Dean album covers (scoring a book of his art at a garage sale), Tolkien tales, and the pastoral musical shadings of Genesis's or Tull's songs of thee woods. The fab four were the first band I could identify on the radio at like age five (though I was maybe confused by Dave Clark Five and the Knickerbockers), and I was handed the Stones' Out of Our Heads LP by my P's with the caveat, "We never liked this," at about age 8 (they'd come around in the 90s and go see them live). Around the same age, my aunt gave me many old LPs by artists like Hendrix and ELP, and my mom's friend gifted me some crucial singles by the Zombies, Small Faces, and later fuzzy Beatles ala "Revolution," which I'd not heard on oldies radio (my folks stopped at Beatles '65 as they said the later era was too drug-fueled). The White Album would probably go on to be the first record that I could sense was more than a mere "album", but maybe a "diverse statement", with "Revolution #9" acting as my introduction to experimental sound collage (well, beyond like the motorcycle revving of "Leader of the Pack", which Eno loved too). My dad did give me the In-A-Gadda-Da-Vida LP and I loved every little part, the phased drums especially (my mom told me that he endearingly made her listen to all of it on an early date).

My pop casually mentioned that a show on PBS (Channel 11 in Chicago) called Monty Python's Flying Circus was a bit like a TV version of MAD or the Marx Brothers (introduced to me at an early age, thanks again, P's). I can't tell you how much the cult TV series fueled my young UK leanings. I reveled in the humor, but also picked up the slang, cultural and historical references (and some more Arthurian myth of course), their bias towards upperclass businessmen (though the mocking of Scotsmen is very unfounded), and their anglo-sense of absurdism (which led to me to the Bonzo Dog Doo Dah band via collaborator Neil Innes).

I guess my biggest walk into English whimsy was Syd Barrett, (and maybe the Incredible String Band, more on them later), and hearing the first Pink Floyd album as a teenager, which naturally was passed over by most of their classic rock fanbase. The childhood-gazing faerie stories of "The Gnome" and "The Scarecrow" opened my Lewis Caroll-ian eyes again, as much as darker tunes like "Lucifer Sam, " or the epic space rock of "Insterstellar Overdrive" (which would inspire a future UK love, Hawkwind). Syd always described the clothes he was wearing, ala blue velvet trousers, wore some eyeliner, and yeah, more or less inspired the whole glam movement via T.Rex/Bowie's fierce love of the cracked saint. Barrett's solo albums also really introduced me to abstract lyrical tapestries that created deep vibes and feeling.

Syd really tied into my late teenage rejection of a lot of very-masculine BS that i never felt much with or was any good at anyhow. At age 19 I walked into a Champaign music shoppe (sadly owned by a less progressive, macho "garage guy") and I heard the most fey sounds waft into my ears, it was Faintly Blowing, by the English band Kaleidoscope, and I think the concept of "psychedelic dandyism" suddenly became as clear to me as that diamond bullet that hit Brando in Apocalypse Now, as well as future UK "popsike" Rubble LP compilations I bought at the shop. The aforementioned corkscrew hair-Joo-brother Marc Feld, aka Bolan, aka T. Rex, and his young malignant mod musings with John's Children, and fanciful folk fantasy with Tyrannosaurus Rex also sealed a lot of glamorous deals. Roxy Music's ironic plastic glam also hit me hard, though I think Vincent "Alice C" Fournier once said Americans didn't get irony and androgyny, only horror (so the AC Band stopped wearing dresses and moved to Detroit). Then-current grungers ala Kurdt picked up the dress-wearing slack, complete with cover of Bowie's ruminating "Man Who Sold The World." Of course, I loved the Thin White D too, and his creation of characters like Ziggy S and Aladdin S, so like most super-anti-heroes, I felt i needed an alias too. Further inspired by wild and unreal rock names like Mars Bonfire, Android Funnel (of a later Arthur Brown band), Helios Creed, I also liked a Daredevil comic villain called Crimewave (a minor guy with a cool purple and green costume, my fave). So my sobriquet was born, which would confuse everyone for the rest of my natural life ("Wait, i thought Plastic Crimewave was your band?" "No...it's me, but you don't have to call me Plastic.") I even thought that like Boo-ee, I might "kill off" this character of PCW and be reborn under another name, but it stuck, as the next pseudonym

I'd pondered was "Astral Spaceways"---but possibly getting called "As(s)" for short did not thrill me (as peeps often would call me "Plaz"). I should add that my Dad ended up making plastic packaging for a living (largely for cookies, nuts, and candy) and once admitted everything he made quickly ended up in the garbage (where I found a lot of my early art).

I guess ultimately this Albion semi-obsession fueled my first Galactic Zoo Dossier magazine, which was named after a then-obscure, non-reissued LP by Arthur Brown's Kingdom Come. The groundbreaking unit epitomized the heavier, urgent, call-to-freaky-arms side of the UK free fest late 60s/early 70s scene ala the Pink Fairies, Family, Man, and the Edgar Broughton Band. A lot of this stuff I was only able to hear via tape trader lists, which was a very 80s-90s phenomena. Collector types would trade often-zillionth-generation tape dubs of rare or not so rare albums. I'm not sure what young-me had to offer these longtime enthusiasts, but I'd hand-write up lists of what I had, and swap about 4-5 cassettes at a time back and forth. One such collector became a good penpal, Hugh Williams (RIP). He knew every psych, beat and prog LP ever laid down in the UK, and I'd even use his clever letter-doodle cartoons in my magazine. I met Hugh and other such traders via classified ads in a reallllllly inspirational publication to me, Ptolemaic Terrascope. Yep, PT was a UK mag that dug deep, along fellow English publications like Bucketful of Brains and Freakbeat (which was visually really inspiring to me). Of course, I also really dug the original UK counterculture mags like IT, OZ, Friendz and Gandalf's Garden, and I still liked American rags like Bomp!, Ugly Things, Outasite,

Here Tis, Black To Comm, and the hand-drawn vibe of Punk!.

Terrascope was uniquely an open-minded beacon into both olden and modern psychedelia, and showed me that doing interviews with these then-still-living legends was possible. I had mostly been writing up nutshell descriptions of old UK dandy-mod-psych bands like the Attack and Elmer Gantry's Velvet Opera, and collaged images from forgotten mondo 60s comics for my 'zine-- so when i heard that the long-lost Silver Apples would be rolling through town, I wondered if i could actually do an interview. I simply called up the club (Double Door) and asked, and it was surprisingly easy--they connected me with the booker, and I scored my first "big interview" (after PT had found and interviewed Apples-head Simeon first, of course). Simeon Coaxe (RIP) was a super down-to-earth, southern gentleman who had great tales of opening for hyper-loud Blue Cheer in Chicago, his chance-paintings involving dropped lemons, his old band with Gary Higgins aka the Random Concept, and beyond. The Simeon interview ran in issue #4 of my magazine, November, '97. This would be both my first published interview and the last self-copy-machine issue (as yeah, the first GZD in 1995 was also started because I was given a contraband, charged-up, copy store card). I have to admit I kinda love copy machines, even the very smell of them (especially before they were digital). The neighborhood Kinkos (and independently run Copy Max, still down the street) in Wicker Park, Chicago, was my second home, where I'd often see "outsider singer" Wesley Willis, rapper Sharkula and other zine-sters like Anya Davidson making their crafts.

Local record stores and beloved periodical shop Quimby's helped me a lot, as did solid reviews (with ordering info) in 'zine guides like Factsheet Five. Phil McMullen of Ptolemaic Terrascope also really encouraged me, and even defended me (along with Byron Coley, another guy and writer I really love) when my first magazine was delayed. (The complaint came after I placed a timed ad in "occasional" mag PT--a word I then adopted from them for my own not-often rag). GZD #5 was indeed extremely delayed, due to a few factors. A proper printer, that a friend hooked up, had let the original art sit in the drawer for a YEAR. One day it hit me that I might never get the pages back, and I'm not sure I ever gave out an original drawing ever again, except to the very-responsible Drag City.

Yes, the beloved indie label, then home to Royal Trux, Ghost, Six Organs of Admittance, and other bands I highly dug, picked up my magazine as publisher. They became aware of my mag via an old pal and collaborator, Mark Lux, who had mailed them a copy, as he had a track on one of accompanying music compilations. These said comps were cassettes affixed to the cover with velcro, and were mostly friend's bands (like Scumkid) or my various weird projects. Drag City artist Liam Hayes aka Plush was a friend at the time, and told me the label liked it enough that they would even consider publishing it (they had released the 'zine Minus Times for years). Brilliant graphics man Dan Osborn commenced on scanning the issue, and figuring out colors for the trading cards (and how to make them bound in the issue and perforated, the DREAM). He also helped me package an actual CD with the issue (high tech for me then, I learned a lot). When the issue hit in 2001, it actually looked like a real magazine with shiny cover, though all of it was more or less hand-drawn. This conjured a term I'd heard earlier via tragic comic artist Wally Wood, who'd self-published some solid comic books in the 70s. He called these "Pro-zines," as yeah, they were professionally printed labors of love, and competitive with any other comics at the time, not just self-made "fanzines."

I'm not sure how I stood along other such "zine-like" endeavors at the time (i think mine was fairly unique in that it had no typesetting at all), but the issue got solid press in high-profile publications such as Mojo, who gave me a page-long interview (I was thrilled it had a bloated-era Jim Morrison cover), SPIN, Magnet, Fader, Blackbook, etc.

The first issue for Drag City also contained more early interview endeavors. Joe Butler and Steve Boone of the Lovin' Spoonful were so nice and keen to chat, despite playing a pretty awful gig at a grungy racetrack with the world's youngest Frank Sinatra impersonator opening (a bold claim). There was no John Sebastian of course, but er, future convicted pedo Jerry Yester, who replaced Zal Yanovsky in the band in the late 60s. Yester had also been a producer for Tim Buckley, the Association, Aztec Two-Step, No Neck Blues Band and done two beloved albums with Judy Henske but he seemed unhappy and unreceptive to questions, maybe it's just as well.

More excitingly, this volume contained an interview with Michael Karoli and Damo Suzuki of Can, who are one of my all-time favorite groups. The piece also started a cycle of real friendships (and even collaborations) connected with the mag. I met the two at a Days Inn that they stayed at after playing a killer show at House of Blues, of all unholy places. I had the idea to play them carefully curated tunes and get their response, ala the pre-eminent avant garde UK mag Wire's "Invisible Jukebox" feature or Melody Maker's "pop stars rate the new singles" features in the day. It was actually a pretty flawed idea which I never attempted again. Suzuki was silent almost the entire time, as he claimed he really did not listen to or have an opinion on any music but his own---oops! It was still all worth it, as Karoli gave such incredibly astute and heady comments, that literally have stuck with me forever. When I played him James Brown (who I was so deeply into at the time, and in my book his bands always had a rhythmic assault like Can) he replied, "You could win WWII with Glenn Miller, but not Vietnam with JB?" Upon hearing Pharoah Sanders, he quickly exclaimed, "Ahh, you can hallucinate into the sound." We really hit it off, and he even promised me a track from his latest band Sofortkontakt for the accompanying CD compilation. Sadly, little did I know, the genius guitarist had brain cancer and knew his days were truly numbered. We'd converse over the phone when he was back in Germany (which was very expensive then) and needless to say, it took him a while to get me the track, which delayed the mag a touch as well. I could be mistaken, but I think the track was Karoli's last official "new" release, an intense fact that I've never quite wrapped my head around, as he is eternally one of my most beloved and inspirational ax-slingers of all time. Karoli told me that he and Damo were the "voyagers" of Can, taking trips into the new music, while the others in Can were old-schooled in 20th century classical composition, jazz, and avant garde music. Karoli was the younger buck who played the rest of the band "I Am the Walrus," which shocked them as to rock's possibilities, effectively starting the band. Later, in a dream more or less come true, i would back Damo in Chicago on guitar, with an all-star band of folks from Tortoise and beyond, he cooked for us, would not discuss what we'd play, and he actually remembered me (though my girlfriend from the interview more, haw).

I'd also interview fellow Germanic innovators Moebius of Cluster and Michael Rother of Neu! (and both of Harmonia) for that #5 issue, and I was a little starstruck as we sat at the restaurant Bite, which existed on the block between the club they played, Empty Bottle, and my apartment. I got a short talk in with Eddie Shaw of the protopunkin' Monks via the San Francisco Terrastock. I more or less covered the whole fest, and the idea of a magazine having a fest definitely resonated with me.

Of course, there had to be some UK artists featured in GZD too, besides features on Jeff Lynne-ian psych dandies the Idle Race and Honeybus, I traded an interview with the overseas Bad Acid zine for an early talk with doomsters Electric Wizard. Somehow one of the greatest rock bands of all time, the Pretty Things, also played an incredible show at the then-new House Of Blues, with an entire SF Sorrow-song suite (the psych godhead) and classic Skip Alan in-the-audience drum theatrics. I was able to talk with their truly beloved guitar god Dick Taylor (who'd been in an early version of the Stones, and produced Hawkwind). So though I lambast, the early days of HOB were obviously not so bad, I saw a killer Link Wray set there (he literally let his guitar feedback the entire time) and they also booked Vanilla Fudge, who I got a crazy interview out of for my next issue. Carmine Appice was so chill, despite having risen to fame playing with Rod Stewart, having a long running column in Modern Drummer magazine, and more or less having helped create the "heavy rock drum sound." Appice actually liked the look of my mag, and bass deity Tim Bogert (also of Cactus!) was surprisingly encouraging too. Bogert told the craziest tales of hotel destruction from the infamous first Zep tour they did together. He mentioned that they were still banned from the Holiday Inn chain, ala the Who, but with the disclaimer, "We're old now and we go to bed early."

In my early daze of Chicago I feel I'd still profit from this burg being a working-class town that loves Anglostuff. Gazing at old 60s-70s concert bills at old venues like the Electric Circus/Kinetic Playground, is to look at a who's who in British rock, both under and overground. I mean, let's face it, the much-vaunted Chicago garage rock sound of the era comes from the UK really, with bands copying bands like the Pretty Things and the Kinks. The Shadows of Knight's two big shots-heard-around-the-garage-rock-world hits were both by Belfast bands Them and the Wheels.

Artists from the other side of the pond that were as profoundly obscure as Kevin Coyne could play in Chicago regularly and have an audience, even in the 90s. Coyne was a big sweetheart, and a true inspiration as a multi-tasking book writer and visual artist. He patiently fielded my questions for my mag about being on John Peel's record imprint, labelmates Stack Waddy (I was almost disappointed to learn the filthy bar band were nice guys). I even got to open for him once, I think simply because I was a fan.

I crashed a soundcheck at DIY venue 6Odum to talk to groundbreaking guitarist Keith Rowe, who I'd seen previously with perhaps-the-first-experimental band, AMM, who caught the ear of both Paul McCartney and St. Syd in the London underground days. Difficult-to-pigeonhole prog bands like the Strawbs would play Chi-towne often, hailed as returning heroes by giant guys in Gentle Giant tees (sniff, my people), so I could interview their flashy guitarist Dave Lambert, who was old pals with Marc Bolan, and had previously been in the beloved UK popsike band the Fire, of "My Father's Name is Dad" fame. I also got to open for the Strawbs on one tour, once again probably because I was maybe the only "young guy" with a band who liked them?

The UK folk scene was really beloved in the midwest, with Steeleye Span and Pentangle records in every cheap bin at the time, so I was able to see genius fingerstyler John Renbourn three times, once with fellow Pentangle bandmate Jacqui McShee (I wept during "Cruel Sister", I'll admit it). Renbourn was a lively interview subject too, constantly rolling little ciggies, with a jolly disposition that made him a lot of fun and a fountain of information (who knew that the Pentangle's symbol was seen as satanic in America, so a Grateful Dead-supporting tour failed). There was veritable Isles-acoustic revival on in the early 00's, mostly due to new reissues and the burgeoning indie-folk crowd then discovering them, via popular artists like Devendra Banhart (we were going to start a band once, long story, but we jammed onstage?). So, I was able to see original Incredible String Band members

Clive Palmer (also of the divine COB) with Mike Heron, touring with Drag City's Joanna Newsom (who loved/played with Roy Harper as well, who I'd also get to see a few times). It was a beyond-unreal experience interviewing near-faeriefolk/OG Cornwall-bohemian Clive in particular, and it would even lead to me doing some artwork for ISB via their manager (who later Wizz Jones told me was bad news, gulp).

It was also my amazing fortune to talk with the delightful and positively radiant Vashti Bunyan when she played Chi-towne. She had great tales of being intimidated by then-labelmate Nico, Joe Boyd, the ISB guys, and beyond. She even let me compile a track from my own bootleg recording of the show (a scheme I'd then repeat often). The ethereal "I'd Like Walk Around in Your Mind" was the incredibly dear-to-me tune, as it was the first song I'd heard by Ms. Bunyan on a compilation many years previous-- so this was one of many full circle moments my GZD magazine would bring on.

Possibly going even more full-on spherical, was one time I wished I had a tape recorder on me, for what could've been the offhand UK rock god interview of the century. Ol' Robby Plant has a well-known love of Chicago (he is often spotted at local beloved spot, Alcala's boots) and he was recording here in the 90s (The Jimmy/Robby LP, Walking to Clarksdale with Steve Albini (RIP), whose studio I was at a few times). I often attended Windy City jazz-venue institution the Hothouse, this time to see father-of-free drumming Sunny Murray, and avant saxlord Sonny Simmons. I noticed the front man idol (in my top 5 with Jimmy M) just standing at the bar, and as I strolled past him to see a friend at the other side of the room, Plant said, "Ah, look at this bloke," and pointed at me to his mates. As I made it over to my pal, I calmly exclaimed, "Um, I think RP is here, and just kinda talked to me?" My pal Jeremy Barnes confirmed this, and would also have some future fame in caterwauling indie band Neutral Milk Hotel and the more ambitious Hawk and a Hacksaw (though I loved his Chicago jazz-prog band Bablicon, whom he told me were influenced by Soft Machine). As we were chatting, we realized the show was not starting, and it was because Murray's drum pedal was broken. So literally, Plant and his crew were soon walking around the venue, asking if anyone had such a drum device. Barnes did, and lived nearby, so he was quickly whisked off by said crew to grab it. So yeah, this left me and just Plant and I standing there together. It suddenly hit me how tall he was, and that he still looked like a rock lion, and he actually started the awkward first phase of our conversation. "Soooo, who cuts your hair?," he inquired, as we both had the curly locks. "Er, I just cut it myself," I sheepishly replied, then there was silence. I did not want this chat to be over, but it seemed to be. Suddenly, I had a thought, and blurted out, "Will there ever be a Band of Joy reunion?" When I mentioned this pre-Zep band of his, his eyes lit up--"Why, YES! I live near the old guitarist, we've been jamming again on like Moby Grape and Love covers." Much like the coded vernacular of comic books I mentioned earlier, the universal language of music took over, and I THINK we then blabbed away for a good hour. Time sort of lost meaning though, as I somehow found myself casually trying to convince him to do an experimental album (Robby: "Oh I'd love to, but my manager would never let me." Me: "YER ROBT PLANT, YER ON THE RADIO EVERY SECOND, YOU CAN DO WHATEVER THE F YOU WANT"). He told me a few harrowing Arthur Lee stories ("He just hung around backstage at a Zep gig with no hair, glaring at everyone, we were scared to talk to him, but we were such fans"), and even some Chicago-centric talk ("Who was that band with all the synthesizers?" "Er, Ministry?" "Yeah, love them!"), and I shit you not, we also talked about cult loner Jandek. Plant, a true deep music fan, had brought up the Legendary Stardust Cowboy, another bizarro "outsider music" Texan that I love (who inspired the Stardust in Bowie's Ziggy nom de plume, and somehow I got a track from the 'Ledge for one of my magazine comps, thanks Frankie!), so I had to see if he was hip to Mr. Corwood Industries—as there was no documentary, live appearances, or any info on the underground and mysterious Jandek yet. Plant replied that he'd heard of Jandek, but never heard his music, and the convo ended when Barnes returned with his pedal for Murray, and the show started (Page did not show up, boo). After the show ended, someone in Plant's camp, maybe an assistant, came up to me and said, "Robert enjoyed talking to you, and was curious about the music of Jandek, could you get him copies?" So yes, after getting one of the strangest requests of my entire life, I dropped off Jandek cassette dubs (naturally along with all my own recordings and zines, which mighta ended up in the trash) at Jam productions, to be sent to Plant. Did he get them? We will never really know. The mystery of Jandek did unravel some at least, as I would later see the elusive and pale legend perform live twice, meeting him, and having the rare dorky experience of getting my records signed

Oddly, that very same month that I had the Plant run-in (June, 1998), I went to meet another hero of my youth, Brian Wilson. I'd rocked the "I Get Around" 45 over and over in single digits, and grew to re-love Pet Sounds and all beyond in my college years. Wilson was doing a signing at a bookstore for his new er, so-so album (and I love his first 80s solo album!) which was marred by locals he was hanging with, as Wilson lived in the Chicago suburb of St. Charles for a hot second. I brought GZDs to give him (I had done a comic strip of his life story in one), but one could only buy his new album, which Brian's handler would then hand to the sunglassed Beach Boy to sign, then hand it you. It was an extremely disappointing encounter, but the friend I was with mentioned that one of my groovy visual artist idols, Peter Max, was having an art exhibition across the street and he was supposed to even be present. So we walked in, and boom, Max is just standing there, instantly recognizable by his signature mustache, and not a soul was engaging him. I could not resist walking up to him and giving him my 'zines, and he was surprisingly receptive and exclaimed, "Wow, i haven't seen anything like this in years!" (The only time I got a better reaction was DJ-ing with Gibby Haynes in NY, he cried "HOLY SHIT!" and tore one out of the bag with a manic excitement.) After a nice chat w/Max and strolling out, once again, his assistant ran up to me afterwards and asked for my contact info. I never heard anything back of course, but I sure tried to pursue this, even faxing his NY office, as being his art assistant/toadie or something sounded like a cool thing at the time. Later I learned of Max's sad final days, the legal battles, and....I'm glad maybe I didn't go there. (Look up this tragic info at your peril.)

In retrospect, I also wish I had tried to interview him, as well as some other English legends who'd pass through Chi-town. I was lucky to see Gong with the near-Angel's Egg lineup twice (no Hillage on guitar, but the godly Steffy Sharpstrings of Here And Now/Live Floating Anarchy band on guitar) at the Cubby Bear, and then front man Daevid Allen backed by the Universal Errors at Schuba's (where he proudly dropped his pants, showing his old man uncircumcised willy). We got to chat at the show (with my lead in being our mutual NY pal Virginia Tate), and I shoulda have rolled the tape, but at least he made out a diploma to me from his made-up University of Errors. That kind of absurdism defined Daevid, as he subscribed to the philosophy of Pataphysics ("intricate and whimsical nonsense intended as a parody of science"--wiki), and whose biography i had poured over. Gong were an ideal band to me, combining the avant garde, space rock, communal vibes, and even pure fun. Allen had also co-founded the groundbreaking and much beloved Soft Machine, was a skilled and unique cartoonist, and showed me that a "rock star" could be irreverent, spiritual and not some destructive/macho "bad boy" (plus Tate told me he loved my favorite comic strip of all-time, Little Nemo in Slumberland). NZ's Chris Knox was another such highly respected underground Renaissance man that I got to meet/see around that time who made a big impact on me, and I wish I had gotten an interview with.

I also got to see Dave Brock's Hawkwind at the Park West and Cubby Bear in the 90s, which blew my young mind. The band had a huge Midwest following "in the day" as they played here incessantly in the 70s, even getting arrested in nearby Indiana. The Ladbroke Grove heavies have become mildly associated with my personage somehow, which I am soooooo ok with. Not only are they the only band I ever attempted a cover set of, a thrilled outfit of mine got to open for Nik Turner's Hawkwind twice— why the hell did I not interview Nik then I do not know (RIP NT). I'd first seen Turner's incarnation of the spacerawk deities in 1994, truckin' up from Champaign at Chicago's legendary club Lounge Ax, with a young Sleep opening, and the show was a life changer. Turner very dramatically took the stage via walking through the crowd in an all-white space suit, and giant face-obscuring helmet. This tour was for the Space Ritual live album's 20th anniversary, so Hawks' veterans Del Dettmar and Allan Powell were in tow, not to mention special guests Genesis P-Orridge and Helios Creed. It was a friggin' happening.

Interviewing Vashti Bunyan backstage at Lakeshore Theatre *(Photo: KA Baird)*

After chatting with Pentangle's John Renbourn at Martyr's *(Photo: Scott Wilkinson)*

Wyld Chicago

I moved to Chicago proper in the Summer of 1995, to the Wicker Park-adjacent Ukrainian Village, ending up right down the street from then-fledgling club the Empty Bottle. My first show there was the Northwest's Space Needle, who smashed a guitar to bits and I nabbed a piece, Blow-Up style. The WP hood was in the process of heavy gentrification, as it had been declared a 'hip" place by various publications, so much so that MTV's "Real World" non-reality show moved in several years later, to much protest (many punky friends would purposely ruin the film shoots, haw). I do gotta say, it was still very cheap rent in da 90s, there were a zillion dive bars and diners, (Busy Bee, Friar's Grill, Leo's Lunchroom), record shops, vintage shops, book/video stores (Myopic/Earwax), and copy places, not to mention aforementioned zine-center-of-the-universe shop Quimby's. There were also loads of open minded/don't give a fuck music venues like Urbis Orbus coffee shop, Phyllis's Musical Inn (which still remains), Big Horse (a truly gnarly place that sold sickness-inducing tacos in the front, and was an anything-goes venue in the back), Roby's (run by an Albanian ex-soccer player and often booked by noise weirdo Twig Harper, so I saw amazing subterranean acts like the King Brothers from Japan and SF mutant art collective Caroliner). There were also DIY experimental shows at lofts like Heaven and Enemy, and the more prestigious Double Door still hosted great gigs like Spiritualized, Suicide and Radio Birdman. The DIY ground zero/grimy venue the Fireside Bowl was also nearby, as was endearing hole in the wall the Mutiny. In my outskirt neighborhood, there was Bar Vertigo and an amazing trans bar called Lolas, that had a silhouetted dancer booth, smoke machines, and mirrored walls (they got the police called on them by a neighbor once ala me playing there too loud once, which was a recurring theme in my life). Club Foot was nearby too, which had great Mod and Glam DJ nights, and degenerate photographer Fred Burkhart's studio on Halsted where wild shows and parties took place was a bus ride away. As was my fave weirdo, pop culture surplus store, Uncle Fun's.

At this time, the hyped scene in the Windy City was arena-grunge-rockist bands like the Smashing Pumps (ok I was a fan at first, and would even chat clothes with old down-to-earth-groovy-era Billy at shows), Urge Overkill (who I oddly did have dancing to a DJ set I did at Delilah's once), Veruca Salt (who would shop at the vintage place i worked at, along with one similarly touted Ms. Phair), and even bands as average as Triple Fast Action and Fig Dish were getting signed to major labels as tax write-offs.

The maybe-not-really-hyped-but-somewhat "Chicago No Wave" scene ran sorta undergroundly concurrent to that glossier movement, but seemed to bottom out soon after I arrived in the city. Integral venues like Czar Bar, Milk of Burgandy, and Dreamerz, that hosted bands like Couch and Zeek Sheck dropped like flies, and popular-type-bands of the scene like the Scissor Girls and Lake of Dracula (a veritable supergroup!) played their last shows in the first few years. Committed weirdo stalwarts like Flying Luttenbachers aka Weasel Walter, Bobby Conn, and Metalux soldiered on, or were reborn as acts like the costumed Bride of No No or Magas (Marlon/Jim of Couch). Still, it might have been ok that this "scene" kind of died out, as it was riddled with heroin, which I believe was also cheap and prevalent at the time. One of my first roomies in Chicago was in a shall-be-unnamed such band that I also shared a practice space with, and I watched him go down hard due to junk, but a few friends got out of the life/addiction and are doing fine, luckily.

I maintain that in the 90s, psychedelia was still a dirty word, equated with smelly hippies and the then-VERY-unhip fratboy-beloved Grateful Dead. So, it took some work to find adventuresome rock acts in the city, as mostly snoozy post-rock (or "post-fun" as a friend called it) and "indie-sleaze" reigned (god, I hate that term). There were a few psych-pop tunesmiths around, like Plastics Hi-Fi and the Joy Poppers (who were great, talented, heady dudes who lived above the vintage shop i worked at). There were a few "space rockers" like Ashtar Command/Sabalon Glitz (both helmed by scenester Chris Holmes), and the truly dizzying Frontier, who really had a profound effect on me. The hard-to-pin-down outfit would often change their sound from show to show, from driving drone-rock to minimal electronic beats, or on occasion just propping their guitars on their amps for feedback (like my heroes the Misunderstood did in 1965). Their gigs were almost always near-happenings with a synesthesia of smoke, lasers, and lights, often obscuring the band--so it was an honor to be part of a reunion residency at Empty Bottle they had decades later. I also would go see locals in the cosmic/improv jazz sphere, like Fred Anderson, Hamid Drake, Michael Zerang, David Boykin, and

Nicole Mitchell--plus the old school AACM crew (Art Ensemble of Chicago gig in '97 or so remains a total immersive fave to this day). John Corbett's nights at Empty Bottle brought in international godhead jazz heavies like Milford Graves, Alexander Von Schlippenbach and Joe McPhee.

Windy Utopia Crashes

My first job in the city was at an art supply store downtown-ish, ordering the very pens I'd use at work to draw my first GZD magazines. The owner was an was rarely around,, so we could do our own thing, play weird music, and I could still look like a freak, as I was wearing a lot of glammy nail polish and make up at the time. The store was housed in the historic Tree Studios building, which was adjoined to the Shriner Temple, where i got to see Bozo thee Clown perform once for free (also like when I was three years old). It was a truly strange and majestic building that looked like an Indiana Jones set inside, with round hallways and swords, and there were also creepy, dank basement-accessed tunnels than ran under both buildings. At that time, it was surrounded by transient flophouses, in a fairly derelict area full of parking lot scams (if an event was happening nearby, a vacant lot would suddenly be $25 to park there). Bizarrely, a fancy chain hotel moved in across the street, and young professionals strutted by to their drone jobs, and it was sure interesting to watch the various populations intersect. Now the place is a wine bar and the entire area is fu fu tourist stuff (though i later interviewed This Heat in a "hip" hotel over there). The cast of coworkers would have actually made a good reality show, as you had: the over-reacting campy manager, the owner's hunchbacked toadie/handyman (no joke), an arty guy I'd met before at a Thinking Fellers Union show, the uptight intellectual farmboy (who did instill a love of Kris Kristofferson in me and I got him into the Seeds), the Wiccan, the hippie, the

Akron kerfuffled mensch, the tough ex-New-York-ambulance-driver-who-got-electroshock-therapy-as-a-kid-for-rebelling too-much manager, the kindly about-to-become-a missionary, the creepy "come to my church" religious guy, the Vietnam vet who still liked to party, the teenager who definitely liked to party, the agro/horn-rimmed/Gwar-loving/90s lady with a chip on her shoulder (we'd hit Japanese noise shows though, like Core/Government Alpha), and even the handsome actor (Clay Calvin, who stayed my bud and I'd go see his plays, as we both loved Can, the Stooges, and Burt Reynolds—he ended up on my mom's soap opera for a sec too!). Despite the store crumbling beneath our feet as the death-throes-of-alcoholism-owner ghosted for weeks at a time, there was a tragedy that severely sticks in my mind today. We had a basement framing shop and a TV industry guy came in once to get all these original pieces of artwork framed up. It was Pedro Bell's hyper-detailed and godly art for several 70s Funkadelic LPs, which I could then see were done in magic marker. It was amazing to even gaze at these, and...heartbreakingly....
(I can barely type this)

the basement flooded.

-gasp-

The holy pieces were sitting on their side in a bin and water went up about a third of the way through them, absolutely erasing the non-permanent linework. Did the store owner call the guy who brought in these pieces? No, she was on a bender and had vanished, as literally hundreds of post-it notes of messages from creditors, suppliers, etc, surrounded her door and desk, resembling a perverse art installation.

Perhaps ironically, my first bit of press in Chicago came in the paper New City, with writer James Porter pairing me in an article with Bell, who had also just released a new 'zine with a lot of his proteges. I got to meet the artistic deity at show once, but he had sadly gone almost completely blind by then.

This was also around the time I finally got a real guitar for jams with fellow art supply store co-workers. It was really just a so-so pawnshop Strat, that i also bought a wah-wah pedal with, as to sound like my hero Ron Asheton of the Stooges, one of the only rockers I was ever too intimidated to talk to backstage at the LA "All Tomorrow's Parties" which I roadied at for Drag City (and ok, him and his rock action bro Scotty looked really sweaty and tired, having just come offstage too).

I mounted a small walkman-sized effects unit onto said ax, so i could alter frequencies/overload with my fingertips, and the jam sessions were soon including peeps from school, and my brother, and we started to call the loose collective the bad-trip-sounding Whispering Trash. My bro worked at a bakery with metal drummer Dylan Light , then-GF Fleur de Polymer, and Champaign pal Ray Donato aka Apocalypse Vision (later of Dark Fog, formerly of avant-emo-ers Grout Villa, and then with solo tracks on GZD tapes as Divis-Ov), so that crew morphed into Utopia Carcrash. We were named after a truly obscure garage band, Utopia Carwash, and I was also really into the dystopian imagery of J.G. Ballard's Crash, and Bowie's salute on Low, "Always Crashing in the Same Car."

We annoyed everyone and reveled in it, as the band/art/noise/whatever collective sounded like five people all playing different songs at once. One of our loud sets got an art gallery closed down, and there was even a claim of permanent hearing damage being caused at a gig at a lil' concrete box called Logan Beach, aka now the basement at the beloved Lula Cafe. Sonically, I was inspired by the more out Velvet Underground or MC5 bootlegs (from "The Nothing Song" to "Black To Comm") to northern UK doom-sludge like Skullflower and Ramleh. I also loved the feedbacking New Zealand X-Pressway world of Dead C and Garbage and the Flowers, and the more experimental "krautrock" bands like Limbus, Dom, and Faust.

I'd heard Faust back in college years, but seeing them at Lounge Ax in 1994 showed me the mind-boggling possibilities of extreme performance. I'd known of Japanese noise radicals like Hanatrash/Masonna, the bloody Viennese Actionists, the Stooges' early oil cans-as-drums/contact mic in blender period, violent artists like Chris Burden, the smashin-up-stuff/"autodestruction" of the Move and Who, and Einsturzende Neubauten's room-clearing playing of heavy machinery and shopping carts, but I sure hadn't actually seen much of it. This Faust performance was truly dangerous, with a naked Jean-Hervé Péron smashing in TV screens (a thing I'd nick later, I'll admit it), and setting a chainsaw loose on an old rusty oil barrel, sending a shower of sparks into the crowd. I would later miraculously get to interview and then collaborate with Péron, and he told me the sparks were harmless, but I'm not so sure!

At the same venue as Faust, ol' Lounge Ax, I also was inspired by Merzbow, which was then a trio-- the shirtless, screaming singer had four nipples (no joke), a lady "percussionist", and main-man Masami Akita (who'd been at this since 1979) scraping what looked like a converted fluorescent light holder with coils (which he held like a guitar). I also saw another beyond-legendary Japanese trio, Fushitsusha at the Ax, for a blisteringly hot three hour show. Leader Keiji Haino played his sensei role to the hilt, threatening the drummer with his cane (or perhaps merely "conducting"?) as the unit dynamically shifted from pin-drop silence to screaming, blackened, apocalyptic fuzz storms.

Coincidentally enough, Utopia Carcrash's first first show was at Lounge Ax, and I always set out to have a spectacle on stage. I'd build sculptures out of old toys and junk that I'd find in the trash, and chop them to bits with a literal ax --once nearly braining myself as the blade flew off straight up into the air, landing JUST next to me). I also liked the wrestling/grunge-rock move of tackling the drummer (dumb, as the hulkin' dude pinned me in 2 seconds once), and I even tried action painting on stage ala my heroes the Creation, but the fumes were unbearable and I felt sick. I was pretty happy to win the respect of an agro crust-punk co-worker when he walked into a gig at Empty Bottle. He grinned and said, "Yuppies were running out plugging their ears, I loved it!" Another co-worker and future rockin' best pal, Frankie Delmane got hit in the head with a flying chunk of an old computer I was chopping up, and echoed this sentiment (he'd also seen bands I loved like Smegma, and had been in death metal bands in Portland, so he could not be fazed). We naturally wore wild costumes, so the glamster in me went pretty wild, aping the outfits of Arthur Brown and Peter Gabriel, but on a budget—though clothes were plentiful from the thrifts (the Village Discount Outlet chain being my eternal fave) and vintage shop I worked at, Dandelion. I'd oddly once waited on Nikki Sixx of Motley Crue at the shop, while working on a GZD page about the early days of Slade and Alice Cooper, and we had a weird lil glam rock discussion. I also befriended Hamish Kilgour of the Clean/Bailter Space there, when I was playing some psychy sounds and he stopped in with his then-band the Mad Scene (with ex-Go-Betweens bassist and Lisa Siegel, who also loved Syd). We'd go on to hang in NY, and Hamish let me use a track of his for one my early GZD comps. The Clean even sung happy b-day to me from the stage once, sniff--I really miss kind, gentle Hamish (RIP HK).

Utopia Carcrash would also grab cheap T-shirts from the thrift and paint on them for our first "Band T's", and more DIY lessons were learned as we self-recorded on 4 track, and then released handmade CDRs and cassettes. Monica Kendrick of the Chicago Reader reviewed such a release and gave us encouragement, exclaiming that it had melted her CD player into goo.

Utopia C mostly played more art happenings, like the underground Moon Fungus Festival (booked by longtime bud Mike Toole) which featured visual art and performances in a heart-of-Wicker building with unhinged hippie rockers Soul Food (RIP Beau, miss you) and electronic droners TV Pow. At the aforementioned Bottle, we opened for outfits as diverse as Marilyn Manson's keyboardist's band (!), Nation of Fear; avant German minimalists Tarwater; and US Maple side-project Robert Johnson and the Browns. Thee Maple were another hard-living band that survived the No Wave collapse, barely—they always conjured the Magic Band covering "Penetration" with a touch of the "indie angular" which was cool by me.

The two most exciting gigs for the band were opening for Bardo Pond and High Rise. I'd met the Bardos at the San Fransisco Terrastock fest (where I saw all from Kendra Smith to Mick Farren, 50 ft Hose to Alastair Galbraith) and they were the sweetest kids, and I'd been going to see their post-shoegaze scree since college. I was always in awe of their scuzzed-out din, with Isabel Sollenberger rising above on cracked vocals and flute (let's face it, every indie psych boy had a crush on her too, and she'd actually talk to you, unlike say, a certain beloved Mazzy S singer). Bardo Pond had a similar free-noise-collective beginnings in their pre-early days, and felt with us I think, as they also had noise-guitarin' brothers, bassist Clint loved comics, and I loved original drummer Joe's dark jazzy vibe. We'd all become pals and I'd go on to stay in their similarly many-years-of-dwelling compound in Philly on many tours--it was always a lovely oasis. I'd play many shows with them over the years, often via side projects like Aye Aye and Curanderos at venues like the Kyhber Pass and Kung Fu Necktie. I'd even release an album from their guitarist Michael Gibbons as 500MG.

The other big show was High Rise. I can't put into words how stoked I was to be opening for these beyond-legendary, underground Tokyo rockers.

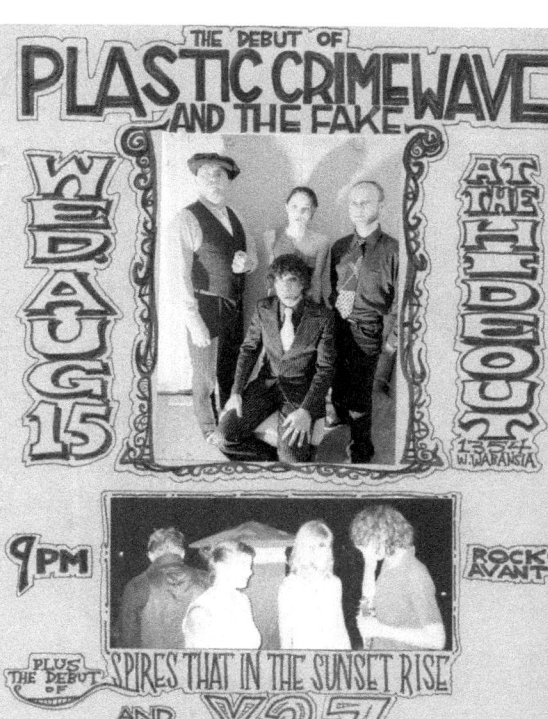

At the airport after the Mainliner/Splendor Mystic Solis tour, Shimura Koji, Nanjo Asahito, PCW, Kawabata Makoto

Psychedelic Ambassador to Japan

Yes, someone actually called me this imaginary title once, and I've been called much stranger and worse things, so I'll take it (with a grain of salt). It all started with the mighty High Rise gig. A friend had laid a cassette on me of the said power trio a few years previously, around 1996, and to say it opened my doors to the Japanese underground would be an understatement. In my mind, High Rise completely changed and upped the game for what might be called "acid rock." The band went back to 1982, formed by bassist/vocalist/svengali Asahito Nanjo, and six-string scorcher Munehiro Narita. Drummers came and went, but HR has always tapped into the molten-hot heart of rock n roll, with their simplicity meets post-everything approach. The intensity of hardcore, free jazz's dissonant maximalism, punk's riff economy, biker rawk's fried-out roadburn, and even black metal's apocalyptic lo-fi buzz all figured into their intense sonic stew. Nanjo helmed other projects I would worship, like Musica Transonic, Seventh Seal, Toho Sara, and too many to mention, as well as running the prolific La Musica label. Dressed all in black, with shades, he was naturally a protege of Keiji Haino, and looked like a cross between Sky Saxon of the Seeds and Sterling Morrison of VU. High Rise led me to the Tokyo Flashback compilations on PSF records, where I discovered many other great bands like White Heaven, Angel in Heavy Syrup, and a then-baby psych-collective Acid Mothers Temple—so long story short, this was a mythical band for me. For this tour, HR had insane free-jazz drummer Shoji

Hano (who played with William Parker and Peter Brötzmann), and at the show Narita had every one of his effects pedals malfunction on him (something I could feel with always). Since I lived a block from the venue, I put the band up, taking them to the mildly gross Wicker diner Hollywood Grill (which is still there somehow) and i THINK Nanjo actually liked my band or at least me, though perhaps he just saw an opportunity.

The demise of Utopia Carcrash is hardly worth going into, as a pretty cliche mix of a personal break up/eternal sibling squabbles killed us, but this glorious high of the High Rise show would also lead to the craziest offer this then-25-year-old could ever imagine.

Nanjo wrote me from Japan to ask about setting up a tour for his new trio, Mainliner, which featured Makoto Kawabata of Acid Mothers on guitar and Shimura Koji of White Heaven and Miminokoto (and occasionally High Rise) on drums. The part of the "offer" which truly melted my young brain was that I could also play in a Nanjo "concept group" called Splendor Mystic Solis. I was not sure how nobody-me added to the "super" of this "transcontinental supergroup" (which Nanjo dubbed it), as the amalgamation would also include then-Ruins bassist Hisashi Sasaki, a musician of the highest of abilities, when I knew like a few chords. The Ruins were an "extreme brutal prog" duo that were beloved in Chicago, as they had releases on the local Skin Graft records, as did other cherished and crazed Japanese outfits like Melt Banana (who I saw probably a half dozen times) and UFO or Die (aka the Boredoms). I once chatted about 70s Genesis for like an hour with drummer Yoshida Tatsuya, who is also the singer/composer of Ruins, ala Magma's Christian Vander. The duo's insanely complex songs covered all from atonal punk to prog bombast.

The first Mainliner/Splendor Mystic Solis first show was 7/17/99 with Ruins headlining (Yoshida would go home afterwards, Sasaki would hop on our tour) and I gotta say, it went pretty fuckin' well! Splendor Mystic Solis raged it hard, with all three guitars stopping on similar dimes while Makoto still balls-shredded, and Nanjo uttered his trademark delayed moans from the void (and also moved to guitar). Nanjo instructed me to play play as such: "Elegant, echo, delay, Syd Barrett/Ash Ra Tempel style" (as we had bonded at my minor Syd shrine earlier). We both spaced out and freak n' rolled in proper AshRa fashion, largely due to Koji's textural but intense drumming, and the audience went kinda nuts!

For the tour, I enlisted old pal T Peterson as roadie/van-supplier, with Nanjo promising to pay for its rental, a good thing, as we were all so broke. Booking my first-ever tour was an education, though, as in those days it was all done by phone. You had to catch the booker when they were in, and pray to not miss their return calls (no caller ID even then either). You could also get stuck with expensive phone bills with chatty club workers, so I'd always have to make sure that NY booker "Jedi" called me, as he told lonnnnnng stories. I was incredibly inexperienced to say the least, so several shows fell through. So, there were lot of "holes" in this midwest to east coast jaunt, a few unrealistic drives, plus no air conditioning in a cramped van with heat-trapping carpet samples lining the inside-- and it was the ragingly balmy

Summer of '99. There was not even enough seating, so Nanjo often laid on top of the amps in the back, which I have no idea where we even got (or the drums). Detroit was our first show, with Universal Indians, and we were massively late and the show was almost cancelled, setting a great precedent for the rest of this mad endeavor. Also, I suddenly began to see another side of my hero Nanjo, who now seemed upset I had not asked for money-deals for each show, when that was never discussed or even considered by this nascent, happy-just-to-be-there "tour booker." Nanjo actually kept telling me that Makoto would be "very angry" if I did not get these $ guarantees, though Makoto was so relaxed and never directly asked me about any financial matters, so I was pretty confused. I later found out that Nanjo had promised him money, but it turned out Makoto was a smart cookie and knew I was an unknown quantity as a booker, and figured it was BS.

Also somewhat distressingly, I heard Nanjo had a wife and family back home in Japan, but he brought along a previously unmentioned young lady on tour, who was my age, when he was 50. Nana clearly was his er, partner for this tour, and would only occasionally sing, as this crew would assume different configurations and play as Okhami No Jikan and Toho Sara on some nights of this "Japanese New Beatnik Tour" (as Nanjo oddly dubbed it). This multiple-but-same-bands thing would almost shoot me in the foot at the Cooler in New York. I really wanted to play the Big Apple for the first time, but famed "openers" Lee Renaldo and Christian Marclay (who were truly nice guys) droned away for like an hour and a half-- and Splendor Mystic Solis was almost going to be cut! I kinda begged the booker Jedi to play and won, whew—ha.

We came back to the Cooler to see another band a few days later, and Nanjo majorly pissed off Jedi, by deciding it was ok to set up his own merchandise, taping things to the wall and messing up the paint in the process. Nanjo also ticked off my friend we were staying with in Brooklyn (agro art store friend who had moved there) so we were ordered to make ourselves as scarce as possible. This was both fun and sucked, because we were stuck in NY with no shows set for days, and I was so broke as we were barely getting paid for the shows. I remember I somehow conjured money to buy the protopunkin' Crushed Butler 10" at Rockit Scientist in Manhattan, though I think I lived on $1.99 veggie pitas that the Wendy's chain had at the time (basically bread and roughage, whee) Still it was fun, as the city was so alive with incredible freaks everywhere, and somehow I had a, er nice rendezvous with a lady on a NY rooftop.

It honestly seemed like every tour stop had drama, a promoter literally passed out under a truck when we played a biker bar in Minneapolis called the Terminal Bar (oh the looks we got when we walked in and Creedence was a-blastin'). The same booker had to break down his own door as to put us all up later in the night, as he naturally lost his keys. Philadelphia, with the aforementioned sweeties Bardo Pond, was so damn fun that I literally forgot my guitar there after a late-night jam session in their Lemur House studio (where are them tapes, MIKE!?). Even then, the next glowing morning, Nanjo was really mad for some reason. I had been wondering why the freestanding speakers in the back of the van were always somehow ending up face down, and I found out why when leaning back to attempt to turn them over. Nanjo began kicking at me while spread out on top the amps, yelling "NO MUSIC" (he had ordered such more gently at my own apartment, so I put on an LP of whale sounds). His heel nailed Taralie, who was driving, and she screamed, "HE JUST FUCKING KICKED ME!!" She was so livid, she truly wanted to leave him by the side of the road, he was VERY lucky she/we did not.

All this stress really came to a head in Cleveland, where the air was crackling with a strange energy already. As we loaded into the cool DIY venue, Speak In Tongues, a crew of homeless dudes and gang members were rumbling across the street with boards and knives. An audience member crushed a 40 oz bottle in his hand during Mainliner's intense set, and bled everywhere. This is also where Nanjo tried to completely go back on his offer to pay for the van rental, so Taralie was even more upset, prompting me to have a heart to heart conversation with Kawabata. "What is up with Nanjo?," I asked. Makoto replied calmly, "Many people hate Nanjo." Then after a dramatic pause, he quietly uttered, "I hate Nanjo."
This is when I learned that no one else wanted to touch this tour, as not only was there no new album to promote or anything, but Nanjo had burned about every bridge in the underground, even stealing some records from a friend in Scotland (which was a really dumb move, as said friend wrote for the Wire magazine who reviewed/championed Nanjo's releases).

Still, in retrospect, i wouldn't have traded the experience of this tour and playing with this otherwise-fabulous crew for anything. Nanjo knew this, and what a superfan I was, and maybe he prayed off this (to little reward). A term I always hear coming out of Nanjo's mouth to this day is "tension," a state in which he felt music flourished (much like the VU used "uptight" to describe their speed-addled, musical-misanthropy). Maybe it helped the incredible music he created, it's hard to say. Makoto enjoyed touring so much, that he went along with this BS too, probably gaining experience for his own Acid Mothers Temple tours.

I came back from the tour fried and weary, and found there was no working air conditioning in my place, which was surely a broke-ass theme of this tour. Another show I planned at Roby's got cancelled abruptly, as they were known to do (they also often raised admission cost as the show eves went on). I was able to quickly set up a happening on the Metalux loft rooftop on the South side, which i have to admit was glorious. Seeing Mainliner rage it against the Chicago skyline at night is a perfect vision I will always hold dear, not to mention getting the band on a local public access TV show. Said show, Chic A Go Go, is helmed by the ingenious Jake Austen, who also publishes the great long-running and ruling 'zine, Roctober, which i often contributed to (for my first ever non-GZD mag cover in 2000). The show has lasted for over 1000 episodes, and was based on 60s local program, Kiddie A Go Go, where little tykes danced along to the likes of the New Colony Six and the Left Banke. Austen really inspired me as a much more experienced cartoonist/publisher/rocker (his masked band the Goblins) and loved all kinds of music, so I dressed the boys up in some of my sparkly robes and the only Mainliner TV appearance was committed to archives. Even if the "performance" was just lip-synched, it's fun to see the band in motion, the in-studio crowd going nuts, and then the boys jamming along to the Standells' "Dirty Water" after their tune, as everyone danced (I got interviewed too, as "translator" by host Miss Mia).

I lost touch with Nanjo pretty quickly after all that (most do), but I stayed pals with Kawabata to this very day, so this all would further lead to a Japan tour that he would help me with in Y2K. I was perhaps ominously told right away that Japan would have everything I ever wanted---but I'd have to pay for it--hmm!

When I arrived in Osaka, I was met by Acid Mothers' Cotton Casino, a kindly electronics-playing lady, who took me to see Makoto play at the legendary punk club, Namba Bear's, owned by Seiichi Yamamoto, who played with Boredoms and Omoide Hatoba. Kawabata played with Space Machine that eve, featuring now-cosmic-minded, ex-noisester, Masonna. He also helmed Christine 23 Onna, a duo with his lady Fusao Toda, of excellent all-female psych band Angel In Heavy Syrup. I got to visit her sweet vintage shop, and the Alchemy records shop (a label I revered), where Masonna (aka Takushi Yamazaki) worked, later in the trip.

More excitingly though, in Tokyo I visited the headquarters of the PSF label, Modern Music. My former collaborator Koji took me there, who I stayed with in a literal temple--I'd hear gongs upstairs at like sunrise (and oddly there were a lot of hamster habitats around). I handed the Modern Music/PSF owner/legend Hideo Ikeezumi the CDRs I was peddling, and I was nervous as he played them in the store to sample them. Finally, he said, "I like, Blue Cheer sound" about one of my projects, and he actually bought a few for the shop—what a relief and honor! I remember seeing a huge stack of CDs being sold as a Les Rallizes Denudes box set, which really made me realize the magnitude of that still-very-secret band. I found some CDRs for sale via Nanjo's La Musica label, and one had a live recording of a Splendor Mystic Solis show I played, so I had to begrudgingly buy it. I'd recorded the Chicago show, and was given another live bootleg from Ed Hardy of Eclipse records. Eclipse was a label that captured the zeitgeist of the then-happening "New Weird America" (as the Wire mag called it) or "free folk" underground of the time, ala Jack Rose, Six Organs of Admittance, Sunburned Hand of the Man, Fursaxa—and even Acid Mothers and Sun City Girls. Hardy also made me aware even further how much of a scammer Nanjo could be, by telling me how much he liked the box sets I was on that Nanjo sold him. Well, first off, "sold him" is a very loose term, as Nanjo only sent the merchandise along when Hardy cornered/threatened him. More distressingly, Nanjo had completely bootlegged tracks from tapes of my bands and early GZD mags that I had given him. The said "box set" was just ten unlabeled CDRs accompanied by sheets of paper, which severely misspelled most tracks with zero information--and then all was just wrapped in cheap plastic (with no "box" to speak of). This would lead to my own "bootleg of the bootleg" version of this set (which I sold a lot of copies of somehow) and more importantly my first ever vinyl release, and "imprint" Galactic Zoo Disk. Heavy Acid Blowout

Tensions became the very-Nanjo-ish title for a live Splendor Mystic Solis LP I co-released with Eclipse.

In Tokyo, I was also privileged to jam with Koji of SMSolis again, and his band Miminokoto also elegiacally rocked a set, with Suzuki Junzo just joining as vocalist. Junzo is a record-obsessed, prolific artist of a mensch that I'd also befriend and set up many shows for in the future. More intimidating, was legendary shredder Tabata Mitsuru of 80s post-everything band Noizunzurli, Boredoms, and Zeni Geva sitting in with me. It turned out he was the nicest, most hilarous guy too, and we'd stay good record-nerd pals through his future stint with Acid Mothers Temple, and I'd stay with him on a future Tokyo odyssey. Tabata also played a dizzying set that evening as Alien Social Dance Party, with fellow ex-ZG Fujikake Masataka, where he used a ton of gear to make his guitar sound like it was a synthesizer from several other planets. A young all-female band Nissenenmondai opened, who blew me the F away, the drummer was like barely five feet tall, but a freaking powerhouse into Silver Apples and This Heat (I must say Japan has the most savagely adept lady drummers in the universe). I also played with upstarts LSD March in Himeji and hung w/ the ladies from Core, who I'd seen in Chicago years earlier. Most interesting, though, was legendary Les Rallizes bassist Hiroshi Nar (RIP) doing sound that night, and he was a real jokester! I was told the man had won a "joke off" contest with Acid Mothers' Tsuyama Atsushi, which was no small feat, and oddly during dinner he mostly asked me about 50s-60s American TV shows like Red Skelton and Patty Duke. I'd go onto interview another Rallizes bassist, Doronco, on my next Japan trip, who was a neighbor and bandmate of Tabata (who knows more about LRD than anyone I've ever met).

In Osaka, I'd also play with anther underground legend known only as Guy, of "Guy Unit." I was told he'd played with Derek Bailey and an otherwise all-lady punk band in the 70s, and he now led an Arkestra-ish free jazz ensemble. I remember he was missing a lot of teeth, but had a Keef-ish rock-cool stance, I loved him! Another younger unit, Aska Temple also played that gig and backed me up for a wild show (I got tackled?) at the aforementioned Bears. Lore has it that club owner/ex-Boredom Yamamoto joined the jam, as it was his birthday, but it was such chaos, I'm truly not sure (saki was had, too).

On the trip I'd also get to see Fushitsusha again as a duo with longtime bassist Yasushi Ozawa (RIP) and Haino helming drum machines, with those big boys of noise, Incapacitants, opening (they'd stage dive too!). I'd get to book/open for my hero Haino later, and keep a lot of Japanese associations going, which was of course, thrilling to me, as I still see Japan's underground music as being on the absolute vanguard, and truly able to transcend whatever genre they saluted, mutated, and intensified.

The only known photo of Splendor Mystic Solis with Nana on vocals, at Terminal Bar, MN.

Hanging in Tokyo backstage after Fushitsusha show with Keiji Haino, bassist Yasushi Ozawa, PCW and Kieran Kelley

Kawabata Makoto of AMT at my pad on our first meeting

Acid Mothers Temple's Hiroshi Higashi, Kawabata Makoto, and Tsuyama Atsushi for solo album session at Joe Cassidy's home studio.

The mural I painted of all Chicago musicians that was outside of Reckless Records in Wicker Park on Milwaukee Ave. from 2001-2016 or so.

Too High Schmidelity

When i came back from Japan, and especially from that Mainliner tour, I learned about the very real phenomena of "post-tour depression" or "back to reality" as I grew to call it. Not only are you not stimulated by a new town/music/place every day, often real life hits you between the eyes and things go very wrong. In addition to no A/C, I got dumped by my then-gal who had gotten it on with my friend, and I was also let go from my first record store job, Quaker Goes Deaf. This saddened me, as the place had asked me to commit to a year there before training me, and I saw amazing in-stores by Fu Manchu and the Melvins at the rockin' shop, where I made many formative purchases. I'd known the cool owner Charlie since college days, but seemingly their spot was cursed, as it flooded multiple times and they could not afford to keep me. More distressingly, I was completely broke. I guess, er luckily, this is also when $10 checks for my soon-to-be-late GZD were coming in as mentioned before--more or less saving my life, I'll admit it.

Before Quaker, I'd only had one more job around records, at the fuck-up-musician halfway house known as Cargo Distribution. They had responsibly run outposts in SoCal and Canada, but the Chicago office seemed to be a stop off for every jamming, doomed misfit to move through. This was my second job that would have made a dang-entertaining "reality show", as we had drunks, junkies, stoners, thieves, faded alterna-rok-stars, crust punks, indie snobs, emo kids, drum n' bass heads, and soon-to-be longtime pals like country star/avant-new wave-lovin' Lawrence

Peters, the previously mentioned Frankie Delmane (whose MC5-meets-Groovies band Teenage Frames I was a fan of before I met him), hilarious rapper EC Illa (who also did a great book), my head-brother Jake Garcia (who'd later join the Black Angels), Ska king Chuck Wren, and my boss Rocco Malce aka Reverend Axl Future. Yep, Rocco was an extreme wrestler who'd come back from matches (involving baseball bats with barbed wire wrapped around them) with scars all over him, but he loved comics, Von LMO, Johnny Thunders, and Roky Erickson, so we got along. He still loved mocking hippies, and in another full circle-ish moment, his New York parents were pals with the Lovin' Spoonful, who remembered "little Rocco" when I interviewed them. Rocco was not so little when he gave me the idea to do "Guitar God Trading Cards" for my magazine too (thanks Rocco).

Unemployed, and looking to stay in the "underpaid music industry," I pestered the local record shop, Reckless. There were several of their stores in Chicago, but the original Broadway Avenue one was where i made formative purchases as a lad by Pharoah Sanders, Wizzard, the Attack, Suicide, etc, and I loved talking shop with groovy employee Henry Polk. The small chain actually originated in London, via Charles Taylor of "lost" free fest group the Half Human Band, and "baggy" psyche unit Brainiac Five. Managers at the shop switched over a lot, but I had the most fun with Ministry/Revolting Cocks' Chris Connelly, from Edinburgh originally, he had started working in the UK shop with ex-Magic Muscle man Rustic Rod (another way underappreciated UK subterranean band from the day). The gig wasn't the blow-off people might think, as it was ten hour shifts on one's feet, and chaos all day long as people with varying amounts of brain cells brought in records to sell. However, this was the era when, as a friend put it, "nobody wanted a record with a guy with a mustache on it." Garage rock was semi-hip, but hairy psych and progressive rock were not. This did mean major spoils, as "'flipping by crass buyers" was not quite a thing yet. We were limited on what we could spend (which was a blessing) but even in the cheap bins there was major gold. I'd also meet record enthusiasts galore (let's not say "collectors" as I did not like most of those) who both worked and shopped there, and had real knowledge. I'd previously been reliant on the tape trader network and a few books, like the Flashback, which would later be waaaaay expanded into both Fuzz, Acid and Flowers (USA) and Tapestry of Delights (UK) volumes.

I'm pretty sure Reckless will be always associated with the still-seemingly-popular film, High Fidelity, which was of course filmed in Chicago, though based on a UK book. Lore has it the character "Dick" was based on my co-worker Kevin, who they got wrong, like most things in the film. He was no sensitive Belle and Sebastian-lurvin' indie rock bedwetter like Dick, Kevin had great taste in 60s stuff, and also had the most biting, but yes, soft-spoken comments about customers. We sure had no loudmouth and snide Jack Black guys (who ok, I met in LA manning the Drag City table at a festival, and he was very nice). We were actually helpful to the customers, whether they were "cool", "normies," or "unique characters," like "Junior" and "Pink Floyd" (a trans/blind former gang member who liked hair metal tapes, and an older Black gentleman who claimed he had been in the band, respectively). Most workers had lives outside the shop even, (like DJ Supreme Court, who had the first happening Soul 45 night in Chicago), had significant others, and weren't pining away for any lost loves as man-children (lots of cool ladies shopped there too, I might've ended up dating a few later, ha). Basically, we never cried into the beers we popped open at the end of our shifts (and beyond).

I say all this, because people eternally walked into Reckless exclaiming, "OMG, Is this where High Fidelity was filmed?" This astonished me, because:

A. the layout of the store looked nothing like the movie's (we were also on store two of three, as it moved a few times, but no store ever looked like the movie)

B. Duhh, there was no real store, it's Hollywood, it's bullshit, helloooo. Yeah, I was clearly a lil' punk at the time, and delighted in telling people that the fake outside of the store was just down the street, and the fake inside was a few blocks away on Division (to horrified looks). The indie romcom of a film only vaguely holds up as a Chicago time capsule, with Drag City doing the excellent music supervision (even placing the records in the movie shop) and many of my pals at the time are in it. I was even called up and asked to be in the Lounge Ax scene, with ol' Lawrence Peters at the bar, Liam Hayes at the piano, an old roomie even walks by, but I completely turned up my precious DIY nose at the offer. Lisa Bonet as a fake precious folk singer, where GG Allin once played, and Hasil Adkins brained Bill Meyer (sorry Bill) with his guitar? Heresy. A production designer even asked to have one of my band's posters to hang in the fake shop and I balked too. The final feel-good/singalong/girl-takes-back-sad-sack/barfo scene takes place at Double Door, which was down the street from Reckless too, a club that I'd get to open for Roky Erickson and Sky Saxon/the Seeds at, plus see the Go-Betweens and Blue Cheer—But glad I did not take part in that either.

Long story short, we actually had FUN at Reckless, possibly too much fun (but I won't get anyone into trouble) so I was offended by the confusion with mopey High F-- if anything, Reckless then was more like Empire Records, bitches!! I even got a mural up in the domed ceiling and had one outside of all Chicago musicians, which got defaced constantly. Honestly, the store and Wicker park was still a bit dangerous then, and we had to be alert and not be too concerned about selling customers indie-cuddly Beta Band CDs. We once opened the store with a pool of blood in front of it, keeping this er "crime scene" intact for police, but they showed up hours later after everyone had tracked blood into the store. Anything not nailed down was stolen, even just the no-CDs-in-the-sleeves disappeared off the floor. In perhaps the most brilliant and brutish robbery I've ever known of, someone once hid behind two dumpsters in the alley and literally SMASHED A HOLE IN THE WALL in the back of the store, making off with the safe contents and more, and others joined suit by helping themselves via the freshly-windowed area. The aforementioned junkie bizness penetrated our world often too, as we had the cops there seemingly every day--we were even nice to Officer Ken and er "Officer Brainwave" (who liked the Doors, can you tell we had nicknames for everyone?). People were always coming in to claim junkie-stolen records, with one particularly sad case involving a bottoming out musician selling his GF's records, including one signed by every Ramone-made out to her. Sigh.

That said, I'd also wait on famous peeps like Parker Posey (who was very nice and liked Bobbie Gentry), Glenn Danzig (who passed on some James Brown records), J Mascis (who endearingly bought the first Chicago aka CTA LP), and Electric Wizard on their first USA tour (they shockingly bought some Hammer horror movies on VHS). Still, getting canned might've been the best thing that ever happened to me (more on this in a few chapters, we're going non-linear here, ok?).

My old hand-written "tape trader list" that I'd swap with fellow cassette-dubbing collectors, it grew to some 25-30 pages long by the end.

Eye Unseen/A Mind Unshown

When my old band Utopia Carcrash split, I decided to stick it out with bassist Ray, and Taralie of Scumkid/Spires had just moved to Chicago and was staying on my couch. As stated, the local "no wave scene" was falling apart, but the OG bands from NY, like Mars and the Contortions still meant a lot to me, as much as "psychedelia." I more or less sought to fuse the two, but be completely modern in an intense post-hardcore/noise way that the Japanese did so well (bands like Gaseneta and Hijokaidan inspired us). The freeform/visionary jams of Ya Ho Wha 13, International Harvester, and the aforementioned Ash Ra Tempel (which I still adhere to, and got to write an essay once for a book on Krautrock) also inspired us. Proto-punkier bands like the Deviants, MC5, and the Misunderstood inspired a serious counterculture vibe, and to spread a bad trip malignance like the toxic colors in an oil spill (or say, Flipper, Red Transistor, and the Electric Eels). I would call our sound "psychedelic power violence" often (the latter 2 words being an extreme noise genre).

I had pondered the name "The Supreme Truth" derived from the Aum Supreme Truth doomsday cult in Japan (cults were a little too big for me at the time, I'll admit). The sect was banned in Japan, though, for infamously releasing toxins in a subway in 1995. The leader's longhair resemblance to my pals Acid Mothers Temple had actually gotten the boys under surveillance and evicted. Wanted posters were still up for members when I was in Japan, so I reasoned that if we were ever going tour Asia, or elsewhere, maybe the moniker was not a good idea (brilliant, right?). This still this did not stop the band from playing a little ditty/dirge called "Trip on Evil" on the local TV show Wild Chicago (who were filming us being filmed on a Chic a Go Go episode in a meta move) to the bewilderment of the host.

I guess our general goal was once again to indeed freak people out, and I ended up getting the name the Unshown from a Buddhist text. When we played our first show (also at Lounge Ax), the booker was Thax Douglas, who'd never heard us. Thax was a disheveled elder scene-statesman of a queer poet, who often read his wares before band gigs. When we started playing, he looked in shock, as I think maybe he thought we'd have a funky new wave sound like Prince. Yeah, at the time, this flamboyant not-Black-and-from-MN-but-Chicago-Polish-Jewboy somehow got a LOT of this "You know who you look like...", including from Thax. Once, an older man approached me, in tears, "ARE YOU HIM??" ("Um, would I be here sitting against a building if I was?" But it was sad to crush his hopes). Literally every sex, age and creed would tell me I looked like one P Rogers Nelson. I have to admit I never saw it, and it got old-- as I'm not a huge fan of the Purple one's music. I at least respected the talented lil megalomaniac sexgod, and would cop to the same loves of Hendrix and Sly Stone (who Prince got 4/5 of his act from). As i said earlier, androgyny was still not cool in the Midwest and around this time I literally got threatened with violence by alpha males every day, so I guess an occasional young lady cooingly exclaiming I looked like Prince was okay in comparison.

I guess i liked velvet clothes and theatrics too

(though never wore assless chaps), but on stage i like to think I kicked things up a notch from ol Princey even. I'd often wear Roy Wood/KISS make up, and sport custom-made ensembles with capes made by my then GF. With Iggy as one of my "guys", sometimes I'd just wear silver hot pants, glam boots, and opera gloves (though I'd have to cut the fingers off to "play" guitar i learned) and a big old medallion.

Taralie had never played drums before, and she stunned crowds as 100 pounds of clobbering fury, often screaming as she attacked that kit. Her hands were a maze of blisters on top of blisters from her percussive assault, which bared a mild resemblance to Adris Hoyos of noiserock legends Harry Pussy. Indeed those two got on like a house on fire when Hoyos lived in Chicago for a few seconds.

I'm also proud to say we horrified fans of the White Stripes, who we opened for at the Hideout. I'd heard them in my Quaker shop days, pitched to me as an indie Led Zep, and was not terribly impressed, as I thought other bands on their then-label Sympathy for the Record Industry were just as good/better. The duo was on their way up, opening a show earlier in the eve at the Metro for Sleater-Kinney. S-K were also at our show, which was filmed for slacker film Power Pad, directed by pal Doug Lussenhop aka Dougg Pound (who'd later work on Tim and Eric's Awesome show). Like a proper exploitation movie, we proudly were the band that the main character watches while on some "goofballs" (and I had to get into character for weeks for a scene where I play a rock star buying drugs). The popular/snarky/faux-edgy 90s indie mag Chunklet were thankfully appalled. In a review, of course praising the WS, they called the Unshown "slutty go-go dancer cacophony," which I more or less took as a positive review, but this lil' feminist/dandy-boy really took offense to our dancers being called such, as they were actually very trained and artistic ladies. I don't remember much else about the show, except hanging on the roof with Meg, and we drank all their beer as Jack was sick that night and ran offstage to vomit (He did give us a typical "nice set" comment though).

In addition to dancers, we'd have guest sax player Jennifer Kienzler, and exotic instrument man Jason Batchko of the Joy Poppers, who played on our unreleased album, recorded in a Wicker Park project studio. I gleefully pushed Taralie to play sax on the album, as it was her childhood instrument. "You want me to play sax for five minutes straight?," she bemoaned. She would go on to completely own that instrument again, playing in a more cyclic Terry Riley style and beyond, with her band Spires That in the Sunset Rise. I also used primitive samples from a handheld tape recorder, including a bit of the jug used by some of thee holiest psych punkers of all, the 13th Floor Elevators. Our album was to be called The Golden Curse, as I literally would yell such things at audience members from the stage at our gigs, often screaming, "A curse on your children's children!" I stopped doing this after a terrible car accident happened outside the Fireside Bowl after a show. An ex of a then-lady had flipped his car over in the crash, and a group of locals unwisely ran into the street to try and help flip his car back over. I'd actually lured out Neil Hagerty of Royal Trux to come see us that eve, with hopes he'd consider producing us, and it possibly could have happened-- if our first non-tour had not gone south.

Yeah, I somehow wormed our way onto a few Acid Mother's Temple shows in LA and San Francisco. It was a great time traveling with young AMT, Kawabata and I made fun of each other's driving (I'd teach him what "air quotes" were, with an example of me as a "good driver"). I also met incredible folks like the previously mentioned Ed Hardy of Eclipse, John Dwyer of Coachwhips/Oh Sees, Glenn Donaldson of Jewelled Antler Collective, and David Katznelson of Birdman records. Sadly, Ray announced he was leaving the band midway through this small jaunt, so when we got back and the band van was destroyed in a crash by a crackhead in dead of winter, our fate was sealed.

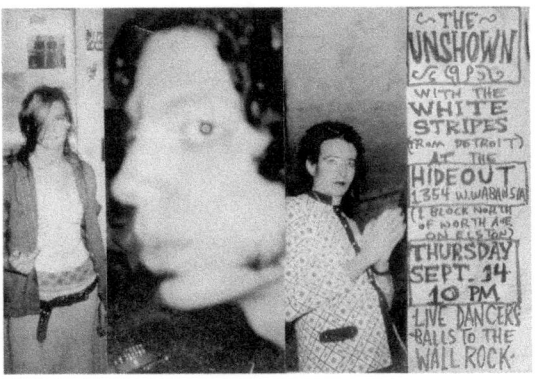

DIY handbill for the Unshown/White Stripes ("from Detroit"!) show at Hideout.

Plastic Crimewave Sound Mach 2, (clockwise from top) Mark "Raspberry Kidd" Lux, Cat Chow, Andrew "Lord" Ortmann, PCW, Lawrence "Skog Device" Peters in the Congress Theatre *(Photo: Suzy "Pod Blotz" Poling)*

Butterflies, Moths and Sounds

After the demise of the Unshown I was band-less, and decided I wanted to record a "solo album" with some little ditties that I even "demoed" on a borrowed 4 track (which were later released on Appollaan Records in the UK as Fire in the Whole CDR, the original working title). I'd always tried my hand at "songwriting" in my bedroom, and I wanted to record some folkier numbers, influenced by the acoustic end of the AshRa/Cosmic Couriers spectrum, Witthauser and Westrupp, the darker Simon Finn, and the outsider simplicity of Pip Proud, (who some described at Syd meets Nick Drake, minus the chops, which was revelatory for me, and I'd get to interview the Aussie legend briefly later). I also had some more electric ideas, where I heard a whole band, veering from droney shoegaze and Swell Maps-y post punk, to Pink Fairies/Broughton-ish riffers. I had a lot of sounds in my head actually, but I had no idea where I'd record an album with loads of guests.

Then a special being entered my life, the Belfast-born Joe Cassidy, fresh off the boat to Chicago.

At a Metro Primal Scream show in Y2K, another near-hero friend, David Baker, introduced me to Cassidy. Baker was someone who understood a need to have a crazed musical vision realized, and was a fellow libra jew. He was the singer on Mercury Rev's first two mad albums, which greatly impacted this author as a lad, discovered via a recommendation in an interview with MBV's Kevin Shields. MR mostly blew up in the UK, who got their truly off-kilter psychedelia, which was very new, but indebted to the old. Baker had settled in Chi-Towne from NY, after recording an excessively brilliant opus under the name Shady, with guests galore. We jammed for a spell, and David was in the orbit of Cassidy. Joe was also just a warm, friendly, charasmatic guy from the get-go and I soon realized I was aware of his work too. Cassidy was the mastermind behind post-dream popsters Butterfly Child, whom I had a Rough Trade single by, as BC had a buzz as part of the early 90s shoegazey scene. After appearing on several UK labels I dug, and following a long journey, Cassidy moved to Chicago after a favorable recording/label experience here, recruiting and endearing many in the local scene. He also had a basement studio nearby in Logan Square, off the Boulevard, so after bonding over thrifting and Syd, he agreed to help me record for the paltriest of sums (even partially trading me studio time for my old Star Wars figures, which Joe collected and surely did not need mine!). The relaxed setting allowed me to bring in my old pals the Spires for sessions, and Reckless co-workers like Connelly and others who played vibes and keys. I also enlisted Philly chanteuse Fursaxa and Acid Mother's Temple on chants and a guitar overdub that was so loud, Joe almost fell out of his chair (he said it was the most deafening an instrument had ever been played in his house). Working with Cassidy was such a learning experience, he'd happily turn a track backwards, add a programmed beat where he thought it was needed, or sample me beatboxing even! (I know, wha?). I pitched the finished album to labels to no avail (though tracks would be released later as a 45 and part of an album). The rockier numbers worked out so well with the rhythm section of Lawrence Peters and Mark Lux, that we decided it could be an actual band. Lux had formerly been in spacepunkers Temple of Bon Matin back in Philly, and we had recorded on 4 track as the spacier Phantom Channel, as we had tried recruiting drummers and other guitarists for years (one was the future drummer from Interpol, can't make this shit up), and Lawrence's fierce metronomic playing had a Moe Tucker/Faust/surf minimalism (with no bass drum, economical for touring too).

I also kinda knew that after having so many old bandmates flake out on me, that I wanted to get my moniker in the band name as well, as I knew I would carry on no matter what (am I allowed to say I proved this after almost 30 years of playing?). Of course, I was also the singer/guitarist/lyricist, though Lux wrote many groovy basslines that we built off of. I initially wanted to call it simply, Plastic Crimewave Band, ala Edgar Broughton Band, but we then thought maybe it was too "bar" sounding. We contemplated a name change every show, ala PCW Quintet or PCW Experience, but ultimately we had to settle on a name to play out. For our first few shows we were billed as PCW and the Fake (our first was Hideout with Spires and no wavers X-27), but folks often thought that was two different bands, so we settled on Plastic Crimewave Sound, after a love of Parson Sound, MX-80 Sound, the original Pink Floyd Sound moniker, hell, even obscure Dutch proto-motorheaders Sound of Imker.

We went through a flurry of second guitarists, starting with friend Caryn Culp, who was a talented singer/songwriter who justifiably got bored with our unchanging Loop-grooves, and next was the force of nature Catherine "Cat" Chow. Truly in her own universe, Chow had a cool, spindly guitar style and her fashion creations were in museums--I even "modeled" some of her designs, dresses made of all-zipper and industrial chain mail on a few runways. I added synth-maestro Andy Ortmann aka Panicsville as our Eno ala Roxy or Ping Romany ala Simply Saucer. Ortmann was a dark prankster of a sound artist from St. Louis, who liked Nurse With Wound as much as ABBA, and I think we met at the record shop, as he was wearing a Skullflower shirt and worked nearby at Kinko's (we mighta traded discounts). I knew he'd be perfect for a hawt gig with Spectrum aka space-deity Sonic Boom at Beat Kitchen (where we'd also play with a reformed Creation to my delight). This Spectrum tour was excitingly dubbed "Songs the Spacemen Taught Us" with former Spacemen 3 man Will Carruthers, and leaned on older S3 material, which had been so huge for me as a youth. Sure enough, Boom and Ortmann ended up talking synthesizers (I knew they would) and I'd play several more shows with Sonic, with er, him once hitting me up for "perky powder" (though hey, this is the guy I saw fearlessly light up a J at Empty Bottle with his Experimental Audio Research project once).

After having out first band photo shoot in the decaying Congress Theatre (thanks Suzy Pod Blotz), PCWS recorded a very-guitar-layered single, "Grade Ceased" b/w "What Goes Up" on a tiny imprint started just for us by record store co-worker Emily "Mother No Head" Easton (it didn't set the world on fire, but Thurston Moore told me had a copy). We recorded it on tape with Kris Poulin at Semaphore studios, housed in the 6Odum venue. We then attempted an album there with his partner, the wonderful Jeremy Lemos (we even named a song after him) who was Jim O'Rourke's right-hand man back then, and now travels the world doing sound.

It didn't work out, so we went back to Joe Cassidy's cozy basement, this time mercifully using very few guests. PCWS's first LP was titled Flashing Open (taken from a sign I'd see waiting for the bus, literally flashing "OPEN"). The platter was released on Eclipse in 2003, and it got some nice reviews in Mojo and the Wire (who called us a "streetfighting Ya Ho Wha 13," sniff) and it caught the ear of Julian Cope. The former "World Shut Your Mouth" popstar had lost his mind a bit by the end of the 80s, creating some truly damaged albums like Fried and Jehovahkill. Cope had seemingly been reborn again as a sort of elder freak-statesman by the 00s, due largely to his Krautrocksampler book, and his Head Heritage festival and website. On said site, he enthusiastically reviewed and posted the entire album (except one mellow track which he made no bones about hating), and singled me out as a "retrofuturistic freak" as I also had sent him my magazine, and tapes/cdrs of side projects, like the experimental Goldblood and Black Hole. The latter was a new-no-wave duo with Rebecca Crawford of the Put a Pons (a band the Unshown played with a lot). BH also recorded with Cassidy and played fun gigs with heroes Metal Urbain and Glass Candy. Cope actually kinda teased me, putting PCWS on a comp he curated for his festival, but we played no such fest. He also vowed to release a live album by PCWS on his Fuck Off and DI label (which we did submit recordings for) but it never materialized. Perhaps most frustratingly, Copey dangled a Scandinavian tour in front of us with his band Brain Donor and our buds Comets on Fire, but instead he took Sunn///o. We'd at least tour the east coast with Comets later, and I'd do a fun west coast jaunt with Comets' Ethan Miller and Ben Chasny backing me (they were way overqualified).

After a great tour with Josephine Foster and the Supposed (the elegaic folkie's rock band), Cat left the band, but would make national news for illegally boarding a plane in 2006. Chow's absence also left a sonic gap in the band, so for our second LP, we of course overcompensated with many guests like the solo LP I'd done before with Joe Cassidy. Cassidy also agreed to record this excessive double album, which nearly killed all of us--literally, as we were mixing the record, someone shot a bullet through Cassidy's door, which embedded itself in the stairs (missing us all, whew). We recorded the entire epic in an unheated warehouse off Lake Street in February, which was not fun in the Windy City tundra. Perhaps this darkness was appropriate, as No Wonderland (the title taken from a paperback book, ala VU) was a doomy concept opus about the fall of humanity—with each LP side respectively relegated to the Earth's formation, domination, future, and then destruction. Each piece also started with a Hawks/Moorcock-y poem intro that I wrote, read by Devendra Banhart, Fursaxa, Michael Yonkers (more on him in a sec), and Chris Connelly. Cassidy ambitiously added strings to "Nill Null and Void" and even subtle/warbly autotune to "Another Plane" before that was really a thing.

The Day the Acid Sky Fell In

One of the more surreal chapters in Plastic Crimewave Sound's time was a tour with Acid Mother's Temple that began on 9/11/01. AMT rocked Reckless the day before, rattling LPs off the walls with their volume, and even blowing up an amplifier (a recording of the set was released as The Day Before Sky Fell In, also on Eclipse Records/GZDisk). Even with this amp destruction in the air (it really smelled like rotten eggs), it was beyond bizarre waking up the next day with my roomie (#100), eating cereal and screaming, "OH MY GOD, OH MY GOD!," as he watched the planes hit the tower on the old Zenith TV in my living room (which my P's got in like 1980). I was literally about to pack up the van for tour with Acid Mothers, which I had worked hard on as the second real tour I ever booked, and one of AMT's first in the USA. I had to ask them, "Well, what do we do, not go?" I got the reply from Kawabata, "We do not care, Japan was bombed many times." So that was that, and off we went, listening to the radio for the dark details as we headed to Detroit. It was one of the many times I played the Detroit Contemporary (ala Mainliner tour) and it was sure a weird vibe, with unsurprisingly not many in attendance. All I can really remember is having a nice chat with opener Matt Smith of Outrageous Cherry and many other hats, who did a great power-psych-poppin' set that night.

We rolled into New York on 9/14, or I should say we stopped and started, heavy on the "stopped"--as the usual nightmare of entering NY was nothing compared to this gridlock. When we finally arrived and parked, it was devastating to see candlelight vigils everywhere on the streets, the endless "missing" posters that were up, and most of all, the giant still-smoking crater where the twin towers were. This was extremely visible from the Mighty Robot art space that we played at in Williamsburg, which was a pretty-legendary second floor loft on Wythe Avenue. I'd say that folks wanted to forget and cut loose that eve, as it was completely packed. Black Dice understandably cancelled, but it was the first time I got to witness the motorik fury of Oneida, who would become pals, allies, touring-mates and even labelmates via a later split 12" on JagJaguwar together. I would also meet Tres Warren of Psychic Ills that night, who we also played shows with later, and would give me tracks for my GZD mag—I miss him dearly (RIP TW). I'd have bad catastrophe luck in NY a few times, getting trapped their for Hurricane Sandy some years later, but that's another book's story.

On a lighter note, on that tour I'd find out funny stuff about AMT, like that synth player Hiroshi Higashi often ran and screamed in his sleep (disconcerting to say the least) and proudly proclaimed that he brushed his teeth twice a year (X-Mas and birthday, i think). Bassist Tsuyama Atsushi was most hilarious man who ever lived (and loved cheap bin records, 8-tracks, and Andy Frasier as much as I did) and the whole gang loved wrestling (I'm convinced that learning this hyperbole-lingo helped them work crowds). We stayed with Mark Gunderson aka Evolution Control Committee, whose pad rivaled mine with an entire wall covered with Whipped Cream...And Other Delights LPs, arcade games, and a "modern primitive" roomie who insisted on doing a "fire dance" for us. "What is a fire dance?," Makoto asked me, and I had no idea. Well, seemingly, it's someone whipping about with on-fire wristbands, while Crash Worship plays on a boombox. We also played with Burning Star Core aka Spencer Yeh at the majestically crumbling Southgate House (though the big draw was an Elephant Six band playing downstairs).

The only time I truly saw AMT angry was in Boston when the label owner had no libations for the band and every place had closed early. "HOW DOES HE NOT KNOW THAT AMT NEED BEER?," Kawabata huffed. We also had no food, so Cotton made us spaghetti with ketchup, it was er, not so great, but very sweet of her, and we lived to see another day.

PCWS also seemed to go through a flurry of second guitarists, so a college friend filled in on a west coast tour with popular indie-art-punk band the Ponys (cool garage-psychsters Gris Gris played some of the shows too). We soon found Nick "D'vyne" Myers via another garage-punk-psych band, the way-underrated Vee Dee. His colorfully monikered band would play a lot of the same events/gigs as PCWS, like the Hozac label's Blackout fests, which featured everyone from Chrome to the Pagans. I think we met at a party though, as Nick had painted the band Crime's logo on the back of his leather jacket, my fave punk unit. Myers fit in well, as he had encyclopedic knowledge of the heavy sounds of Detroit, Australia, UK, and beyond. Lux said that Nick "made us sound like a real band" with his Thunders-ing rock n' roll chops, and he was right. With Myers, we played some really fun festivals, like the much-missed Arthur

Magazine's second LA happening (with Om and Mike Watt playing before/after us), the Terrastock fest in Louisville (alongside Yo La Tengo and Simply Saucer), and a Providence freakout on 06/06/06 (where kids went nuts during White Mice and were climbing in the rafters and pulling out pipes). The first album with Nick was the CD-only Painted Shadows, on the Italian A Silent Place label, who actually gave us money to record (I think the only time that ever happened) but they went belly up after a warehouse flood, and the promised vinyl edition never materialized. Myers added a lot, via his ability to both rock and space out, and he even laid down thuggy background vocals. A self-tiled Eclipse LP with Myers would be the last outing for the band, recorded by John Dawson in a studio in Bloomington, Indiana, that was co-owned by Paul Mahern of the punk legends the Zero Boys and John Cougar's lyricist (no joke). We'd also play great gigs with deities like Trad Gras Och Stenar (all original lineup), Max Ochs, and Rocket from the Tombs, but the band still kinda ran out of steam. Nick eventually left, so my brother was added, and then Lux quit on the morn of a two day gig-run, so we played a very strange bass-less show with an even stranger Arthur Lee-less version of Love. Originally this show was supposed to be "66 reunion" tour of the Electric Prunes, the Seeds, and Jerry Miller of Moby Grape, but the latter three all canceled (well, Sky Saxon of the Seeds passed). We added my talented then-partner Libby Ramer on keys and played a shaky set that some guy in the crowd declared sounded like the Beatles (boy, did it not). Libby and I would go on to start the punk-proggy trio Moonrises (who did two

LPs) with free-jazzy Ben Billington on drums, and we toured Europe and Holland with our ambient side project Solar Fox.

After quickly adding new bassist John Brearly and his wife Betty Eo on synth, PCWS's last tour was with Japanese double-drummer band Marble Sheep. MS was also a PSF Records band I was exposed to years before, helmed by Ken Matsutani of Captain Trip records (who did archival releases by the Deviants, Ya Ho Wha 13 and many more) and they were a hella fun crew to travel with. Opening our tour send-off show was young psych-upstarts the Great Society Mind Destroyers, led by Cosmik Jru (aka Andrew) Kettering. When Kettering's other band Les Strychnine broke up, I swooped in and grabbed him and drummer Karissa Talanian as the rhythm section for a new band amalgamation, Plastic Crimewave Syndicate (the latter word sounding a bit like Strychnine to me), which continues to this day, recording several albums for UK labels like Swordfish and Cardinal Fuzz. The lineup shifted to include drummer Jose "the Beast" Bernal, formerly of Bionic Cavemen, and bassist Rob Rodak of desert rockers Dead Feathers. PCWSyndicate would amazingly open for heroes like Loop, Acid Mothers, Chrome, Josefus (the legendary 70s band did their only shows outside of Texas with us), the Mothers of Invention's Don Preston (who I think hit on a PCWS member), and vintage Ohio cult-rawkers Poobah. PCWSyndicate would also seemingly play every "psych fest" in the land (as psychedelia is now a cool and established genre, ryte?) from Portland, Seattle, Columbus, to Milwaukee Psych Fest, to my own Million Tongues festival with Keiji Haino (who I got to entertain back at my place with "acid folk" records he requested, and I stumped him on one, whoaaa!)

Flyer for Million Tongues 5, 2008

Millions of Tongues

Back in that pivotal year of 2004, when I was just starting up Plastic Crimewave Sound, I mentioned one of the best things that ever happened to me was getting canned for vague reasons from the record store. I haven't worked a day job ever since, and collecting minuscule unemployment money at first really allowed me to focus on my bands, art, writing-- and my own festival (let's call it "the dole"). I had always dreamed of doing this, having witnessed the Table of the Elements fest in 1996, with Tony Conrad, John Fahey, Fushitsusha, Faust (who yeah, I saw like 4x), Bruce Gilbert of Wire. (Wire were also one of the best band "reunions" I ever saw and they played no hits.) I thought Chicago would be rampant with amazing happenings after this, but there was this utter vacuum of similar-vibed avant/psych/folk fests. I'd seen deities like Tom Rapp play at the Boston Terrastock, and I'd also been privileged to witness and then play at the End Tymes fests in Minneapolis. I stayed with promoter Clint Simonson and even got to hang out with drone titan Tony Conrad, UK folk goddess Bridget St. John, free jazz savant Arthur Doyle, and Donald Miller of snuff-jazzers Borbetomagus. I played the following year (as did the Boredoms and Rusted Shut) in "supergroup" Scarcity of Tanks, helmed by Matthew Wascovich. "Wasco" was the sorta-head of the Cleveland freak-scene, booking all my band's shows there (usually with beloved and crazed buds Puffy Areolas and/or Terminal Lovers also playing in some form) at places like Pats in the Flats, Church of Ayler, and Now That's

Class (which had skate ramps set up indoors, a great jukebox and once we did not know we were playing a wake there). Wasco and I managed to convince Nashville's Chris Davis of the Cherry Blossoms, Steve MacKay, and Michael Yonkers to sit in with us. Now, MacKay was my sax-skronk hero from perhaps my fave rock LP of all time, the Stooges' Funhouse, and I'd go on to book him for my own fest---but Yonkers was a truly special being.

I'd been exposed to Yonkers' ingenious, homespun folk LP, Grimwood, at the record store, but then later hearing a few very-electric tracks was revelatory, on a compilation of MN's Dove records (home of beloved garage band CA Quintet, whom Michael was friends with). The unhinged nature of said tunes had me assuming Yonkers was some PTSD 60s Vietnam vet or other such casualty. When I heard the fuzzed, out-there aggression of his shelved 1968 LP, Microminiature Love, via Simonson's Destijl label, I was astounded further--as it basically sounded like ferocious post-punk, but this was of a pre-punk vintage.

When Mike Donovan of Sic Alps (who I'd played with and ridden in the cab of in SF ages back) pointed out Yonkers to me in the crowd of End Tymes, I absolutely had to go meet him. Of course, Yonkers was no damaged headcase, but beyond friendly and gracious, and he slipped me a then-current CD, It's Only Yonkers, which was distorted and skeletal blues rock he had home recorded. I managed to release it on LP via my GZDisk vinyl imprint with Eclipse, and a stray track became a split 45 with Plastic Crimewave Sound, which thrilled me to no end. This would begin a long association for us, as we then recorded a full LP together, Bleed Out, with Joe Cassidy once again at the controls. The B-side was actually a live blown-out document of a noise jam we did together at my first Million Tongues festival in 2004 at Empty Bottle.

Yonkers had not played out of the Twin Cities area much because of health problems, so it was very special to have him, and the jam with him and my band (and White Light's Matt Clark) only happened because PCWSound were supposed to back Deviants front man and counterculture author Mick Farren, who canceled last minute. PCWS did an abbreviated Farren-tune set, with locals like Chris Connelly and John Battles filling in, which sounded great! So, in the end, maybe this was all ok, because somehow I had decided to make the first Million Tongues FIVE DAYS—I have no idea how anyone involved thought this was a good idea. I did get sponsorship and CD compilations made of the artists for the first two Million Tongues, via Arthur Magazine, who I did art and writing for, and even helped deliver the periodical. The fest name came form a lyric in a COB/Clive Palmer song, and I was somehow indulged to invite 3 ½ japanese bands. Kawabata backed by Seattle's Kinski was a no-brainer, but we also flew in the aforementioned Nissenmondai who I played with in Tokyo. Their manager who came along ignored my request that they play no more local shows, as they in fact, played like five. This really ticked me off when a friend (who was not at my fest) asked me, "Do You know this Japanese band who played at....? They were awesome!" We also flew in PSF luminary Jutok Kaneko of Kousokuya (Haino stated he had "original rhythm") who was woefully in a sad state of health (and passed away a few years later), and upstarts LSD

March, who absolutely slayed in a white heat psych-n-burn display.

It was also thrilling to have the mysterious Simon Finn at my first fest, whom I'd gotten in touch with via Current 93's David Tibet. I'd been in love with Finn's lone LP, Pass the Distance, since receiving a cassette dub in tape trader days. Friends and I would pontificate on what Finn's story was, as his LP contained the darkest of opium den vibes. It turns out that the UK-raised Finn was living in Montreal, and was the sharpest, wittiest chap, much like Mr. Yonkers.

With subsequent fests I'd also not be disappointed by my heroes, Tony Conrad, who literally helped name and incubate the Velvet Underground, was a loveable mensch (one friend called him the "happy/sad Bill Murray of drone") who endearingly needed a place to stay last minute, despite me asking for months. That was mercifully solved when my compatriot Ben Vida (who was in a large spacey ensemble I played with, DRMWPN, aka Dreamweapon/ex-Town and Country) offered a guest room. Raga guitar warrior Peter Walker was thrilled to get late night tacos after playing MT, while telling me great tales in his thick east coast accent about Karen Dalton (whose guitar he had with him) and his mentor Sandy Bull, for a GZD interview. He crashed in my "guest room" as did MT-alumni Terry Reid, who was the loveliest chap with no rock star airs, despite turning down Led Zeppelin and Deep Purple in the day for the vocalist slot. Naturally, he had great stories about Richie Havens, Keef and the er Altamont tour he dropped off of just in time—not sure why I did not get the tape recorder out for that one! I guess a lot of crazy deities have stayed in my extra room, as I was in my pad over 25 years (it has been in some photo shoots and such for its walls-covered/festive qualities). God of Krautrock, Mani Neumeier of Guru Guru was one who stayed with me when he passed through--and I did get a great GZD interview out of him too.

Ruthann Friedman, writer of the Association hit "Windy" and one of my fave femme-folk lps, Constant Companion, had a daughter going to school Chicago, so she graciously played MT (I also booked her another gig with a young Angel Olsen, whom I drew an album cover for and supported early on). Friedman had incredible tales of hanging with Jefferson Airplane, Zappa, Crosby, and beyond, and we'd also have fun hangs in Los Angeles/Santa Monica when I'd come visit.

In LA, I also met Djin Aquarian aka Joel Schlofsky of the Source Family/Ya Ho Wha 13, and managed to get the full band to play MT, but that was a bit of mess—as bassist Sunflower, drummer Octavius, and Djin almost got into a fist fight in my living room. Yeah, Djin could be a pistol, though he was the subject of one of the first Guitar God trading cards I ever drew, and a former Chicagoan-- we could get along on many levels, and not on several others. We would go on to record and tour together, but the "hippie cult thing" would often rear its' head. Our association ended when a drugged and quite feral boy attacked my guitar pedals at a show at his "temple" (really more of a shed) in Mt. Shasta, California. This kid went berserk, knocked over gear, got naked, and was subsequently hog-tied (by his dad-of-the-year!) and then was chanted over, in an attempt to calm him (guess what, it didn't work).

There were other minor disasters that would

plague Million Tongues, having Whitehouse play in 2005 was problematic, as they blew a power converter at soundcheck and I had to go bike in the rain to get another one. I had friends work security, as the sadomasochistic noise outfit was known for instigating violence at shows. This was indeed needed, fake security laminates and all, as a lady in the crowd started attacking and punching people randomly and had to be escorted out. Josephine Foster played her delicate sounds afterwards, and delighftfully told the charged up audience to "Shut the F Up". (Something I would often do as well.)

UK folk guitar demigod Bert Jansch was one such case, as I was not going to stomach any chatter for this special performance. Still, a superfan kept yelling that he wanted his guitar pick, and Jansch merely replied, "But I'm using It." Jansch was a very deadpan but gentle soul, and of course the Empty Bottle light rig went berserk during his calm and melancholic set.

Longstanding and gruff UK troubadour Michael Chapman (I believe on his first-ever USA tour) almost got arrested on my porch for the second MT. It seems someone called the police on him as a suspicious character (I was out meeting Ed Askew at the airport, so he was merely waiting). He charmed the cops who showed up, as only kindly Michael could. Guitar god and longtime friend Jack Rose (RIP) also played the fest, and we looked at each other with astonishment as Chapman used his ring as a slide. Afterwards, a lasting and even collaborative friendship between the two guitar gods resulted.

The aforementioned Ed Askew was another mysterious figure to me, that Simonson hooked me up with. The Cambridge-now-NY folk singer of the gorgeous Ask the Unicorn LP on ESP records (my favorite label) now had bad tendonitis, so he could play only keys rather than the stringed tiple he used on the album. Six people hauled a huge piano on the Empty Bottle stage for him to use, which was still not easy.

The Japanese art-punk band, Up-Tight, also had visa problems and only the drummer made it into the USA, he was not thrilled to find out his bandmates were sent back.

Joe Cassidy and Michael Yonkers

Backstage at Million Tongues with Bert Jansch, Million Tongues 3, 2006

The first Secret History of Chicago Music strip from 2005 in the Chicago Reader was on Phil Cohran, but this was an updated, wordier column for when he passed in 2017.

The Secret History of The Secret History

That fateful firing in '04 also allowed me time to propose a regular feature to the Chicago Reader, the city's longest running alternative weekly since 1971. I'd slowly been noticing that I had town pride (who knew?) as I was covering more heady Chicago sounds in my GZD magazine, like the Lemon Drops and Baby Huey. Those very columns became prototypes that I submitted when the Reader placed an ad saying they were looking for comics. Initially pitching it as more of a page-long "info-strip," the current editor did not go for my Secret History of Chicago Music idea. I tried again with the next editor, Alison True, who worked with me to develop more of a trading card format --though it has since ballooned into more of a long column, thank to a synergistic relationship with my longtime editor, Philip Montoro. The first artist that I covered for SHoCM in 2005 was Kelan Phil Cohran, a hero of the highest order, and epitome of all that is soulful and innovative about Windy City music. Cohran started the groundbreaking Artistic Heritage Ensemble (possibly the first "soul jazz"), played with the Sun Ra Arkestra, and through his Affro Arts center on the southside, cultivated the careers of early Earth, Wind, and Fire and Chaka Khan. Cohran was someone I continued to champion as SHoCM grew, booking him to play at an art exhibition centered around Secret History at the Museum of Contemporary Art in 2010. When SHoCM became a concert series at the Hideout, he also played a sold-out show, and he even appeared on the Chic A Go Go series for some Secret History-themed episodes that I hosted.

I also was able to book Ono for said local TV show, and this is one of my proudest achievements, believe it or not--as it led to the reformation of one of the greatest bands that ever was. I'd gotten Ono's 1983 album, Machines That Kill People, from a record dealer in college, who assured me it was "psychedelic"---and it sure was, times about a thousand. I used to describe Ono as Chicago's funky Throbbing Gristle, but that simply does not do them justice. I tried for years to track down the singer, only known as Travis (it's legally so, seen his personal checks) and upon reinvestigation, I found his site, and realized we had been in a Sun Ra-themed art show together. Travis is a total genius, and perhaps the best performer I have ever seen (he loved Iggy too, so often in dresses and opera gloves)--you should look up, as his life story is too intense to be told here, we'll just say his memoir would be far better than mine. After I found Travis, it was then revealed that Ono's leader, P.Michael, LIVED THREE BLOCKS FROM MY PAD, though he moved shortly thereafter (giving me his incredible record collection too). I'd end up booking Ono countless times, and they'd play in my guitar orchestras (known as Plastic Crimewave Vision Celestial Guitarkestras, which featured up to 100 guitarists, no kiddin'). I'd also sit in with them on occasion, help get their two LPs reissued, and I'd simply marvel at their momentum, as this band that never toured out of Chicago was suddenly playing big festivals everywhere, and young kids looked up to them as contented-freak heroes.

I'd also end up collaborating and being pals with (and getting sick records from!) Bil Vermette, who played gigs with with Ono in the day as part of synthesizer collective VCSR, who I also helped get some material released via an archival LP with Permanent records (as well as Bil's excellent 1984 private press LP, Katha Visions). SHoCM also led me to end up booking and playing with the kindly avant genius Vyto B (RIP) and Edward M. Zajda, whose 60s music concrete LP I worshipped for years. I tracked him down via phone in nearby Berwyn, where he still had an incredible shag-carpeted basement studio that my duo Solar Fox would record in. I guess it hit me early on that Secret History could really have an impact, and even birth some friendships. The Little Boy Blues' Jimmy Boyce literally knocked on my door after covering them, and after writing up another garage group, the Knaves, I heard from almost every single member of the band. It also had not occurred to me that people would write me about covering their own lost bands, or their friends. When now-love-her-like-a-sis Annette D'Anna dropped off a package of her old chums the Vertebrats' recordings (with liner notes!) I realized how much easier this could even make my job. I'd also end up releasing archival LPs by some SHoCM subjects via my Drag City imprint, like two volumes by the glam-punk-malcontent JT IV, and a lost album by the rustic Stumpwater.

Poster for the launch parties I curated for Gorilla Perfumes Volume 3 line from Lush Cosmetics, entitled "Death, Decay and Renewal"

Corporate (UK perfume) doesn't suck
Anglodelia Pt 2

In an attempt to make this anecdotal volume go truly full circle, it hit me by this final chapter that there seems to be a sort of theme here.

Quite simply, and perhaps a bit cliché: "Following your passions can make friendships/opportunities/dreams come true"

An example:

I played the Diamond Days festival in New York in 2007, getting together a loose ensemble called the PCW Expanse. I recruited my pals the Spires once again, Virginia Tate, and old NY pal Adam Otracina on drums. The set got recorded, but I barely get paid, and some performers got completely stiffed by the promoter, who vanished towards the end.

Tate gave the recording to her friend Matt Shaw of Appollaan recordings in the UK.

Shaw wanted to release the recording on his small, handmade, very underground CDR label.

It then turned out that Shaw got in on the ground floor of a killin'-it company I'd never heard of, called Lush Cosmetics, based in Poole, England. With nearly a thousand shops all over the world, they sell all-natural soap, beauty products, and perfume.

Shaw then asked if I'd like to draw a comic book-like catalog for their perfume line, then called Gorilla Perfumes. Art from this periodical would soon be on the actual perfume bottles.

After flying over, I hit it off with the company owner and music fan Mark Constantine. I even passed an impromptu "prog rock quiz" that he gave me. I THINK he was impressed as a very-jet-lagged me got them all, from Sallyangie to Curved Air, as he played bands off his laptop.

Then BOOM, suddenly I was some kinda "art star" in this enthusiastic culture of Lush, and I had a whole other life in the UK that hardly anyone knew about back in the states--as I flew over about every month for new projects like painting up storefronts and a van (!), and even drew a complete graphic novel. So, more or less, my childhood Anglodelic art dreams had come true.

I even had a regular spot I could stay in London, via a cool, kindly couple I drew a wedding invite for, so these were yet more friends made via my art. Tristian and Juliet had seen my magazine and lived in Putney, right by the historical Half Moon Pub (where folks like Jansch and Steeleye Span played in the day), the best comic shop on earth (how i miss you, 25th Century Comics), and the Railway, where the Police played their first gig with Skrewdriver! The pub had now been taken over by the Wetherspoons chain, but the characters that hung out there were unreal. Marc Bolan's car crash/death site (with a memorial shrine) was within walking distance too, and I went a few times.

All this Lush action would even allow me to do some instore mural artwork in Japan, where I got to do a second tour, and I'd make more friends/music collaborator pals for life, like Erica Vega and the Flexibles' Andrew Paine--who introduced me to his partner, Frances McKee of the Vaselines (who I saw Nirvana cover as a youth) and we all played a fun show together even.

But to go "fullest of circles" once again, when I

was on all these UK Lush trips, it enabled me to look up and interview my highest-echelon musical heroes.

One of the first I reached out to was Peter Daltrey of Kaleidoscope, whose sounds changed my life as a dandy lad. I met him at his home in Wiltshire, and he took me to Avebury, an ancient site of stone circles and leylines that he said was more impressive than the nearby Stonehenge. I got an incredible interview out of him, and the man brought us snacks and drove us to the next town, what a prince! Later on, I talked him into reading a poem for my belated solo album, which was a mix of then-current tracks and older ones recorded by Joe Cassidy. Terrascope editor and near-mentor Phil McMullen lived nearby, who I had not seen since Terrastock fest days, so I stayed with him and saw his amazing new/old printing press (which he now prints the Terrascopaedia mag on, which I often contribute to).

On these Lush trips I would get around to other activities, and a fun one was DJ-ing with famed fellow head Cherrystones aka Gareth Goddard. We'd only corresponded in the past, so it was fantastic to spin sets together on NTS radio, but the most fun was playing records in a grimy club in still-not-gentrified Dalston. These nights were WILD! I've DJ-ed everywhere from Japan to NY to LA, and it was nothing like this, people cut MF'n loose in London, dancing on tables, loads of PDA out on the dance floor, and dudes screaming at me, "GIMME THAT PSYCH!!" while air guitar-ing. I also saw the worst knockdown, drag-out, savage lady fight of my life there. Even seeing much gnarly shit in Chicago, this was not quite my world.

I kept racking up interviews too, Brian Godding

of godly freak rockers Blossom Toes (RIP), Martin Carthy of Steeleye Span/Watersons, Alisha Sufit of eastern psychsters Magic Carpet, and Canadian folksinger Bonnie Dobson who was living in London (I'd done "Astral Folk Goddess" trading cards for both in my magazine). One of these very same cards was slipped to its' subject via a friend, Fairport Convention/Trader Horne's Judy Dyble, one of my fave cut-glass UK singers. I was then able to meet up with her for a chat in Oxford, and we also struck up a friendship and would have tea upon return visits. The sweet lady also miraculously recorded several layered vocals for my said solo album, Feathered Serpents, released by Sunstone records in the UK in 2017. To support this solo album I got to tour the UK again, with my partner/flute accompanist, Sara Gossett, who played on the LP. One of the best shows of the jaunt was at the legendary Betsey Trotwood in London, playing with the acid-folk legend Mark Fry, whose only USA appearance was playing my Million Tongues fest. This tour led to us playing as a more proper cosmic duo called Spiral Galaxy (who yes, got to open for and collaborate with Faust as mentioned, for another spherical moment).

Also appearing on this very same "solo" record was Bobbie Watson and Jon Seagroatt of Comus, the original UK "folk horror" band, if you will. Their acoustic songs about killing Christians were intermingled with true beauty--usually courtesy of young Watson's sweet vocals (over the feral Roger Wootten). Seeing an entirely reformed Comus play their 1971 LP, First Utterance, at Islington Hall (where I sadly missed a reformed Kaleidoscope) was a life highlight, as was interviewing the whole Comus crew and opening speaker Shirley Collins. Often called "the first lady of British folk", it's hard to describe the feeling as we met and she hugged me! This voice of the ancient isles has given me comfort and pure shivers so often on recordings (especially Folk Roots, New Routes with Davy Graham), that it was beyond incredible to hear her stories, especially traveling the USA as a young lady with folk/blues field-recorder Alan Lomax. I'd strike up a meaningful friendship with Bobbie and Jonny as well, often staying with them in their abode near Banbury, north of London. Seagroatt is Watson's husband, and was newer to Comus, both filling in sonic holes and recording the band, and he had been in 70s proto-noise-rock band Red Square, who only released a few cassettes. I was able to get an archival LP in motion of Red Square, via another imprint of mine, Galactic Zoo Archive, which was in conjunction with excellent and prolific reissue label Guerssen records, based out of Spain. Red Square guitarist Ian Staples still lives near the couple on a groovy houseboat, and was simply the coolest guy, with psychedelic posters on his walls, and a proclaimed love of Captain Beefheart and the Art Ensemble of Chicago (sniff).

Staples told me he got high with my hero Edgar Broughton under a table once at a gig, which is hilarious, as Broughton also loved Beefheart--- and he is another hairy face on my personal Mt. Rushmore of rawk. I somehow made contact with Broughton and he agreed to meet as St. Pancras station and I thought he said on the phone, "pan crustacean," which endlessly confused me. I managed to meet the legendary free-fest insurrectionist at the bustling stop, as he was coming from playing a gig, with an amp on his back and guitar. Broughton still has a punk/DIY ethic (which he all but pioneered in the early 70s) and will play about anywhere for what the booker can afford on a sliding scale ("a day's wages" is all he asks). I was somehow able to cajole Broughton into such a gig for Lush, when the company asked me who I wanted to perform at a launch for the next set of perfumes I had done artwork for. This was my most decadent and indulged period at the company I'll admit, as literally a Gorilla Perfumes shop opened up in the fanciest part of Islington, with my art and logos all over every item for sale—including a double LP that they let me curate, and Broughton even gave me an unreleased track! What did all this have to do with perfumes? Well, these were not your average scents, this was scent as art, as the line was called "Death, Decay and Renewal," so i even got a track by Ono on the said 2LP platter.

For the bigger launch event, which was at an art opening at a gallery in Soho, I was able to get some of the folks from Comus to play as Cominus (Cominus, gettit? great one, Bobbie) and....I asked for my hero of heroes to play, Arthur Brown —AND IT HAPPENED! I even got to musically-open this event with a project of mine, and yes, naturally interviewed Sir Lord Brown.

It was slightly awkward to hand him my magazine, its title boldly ripped off from...er, in homage to one of his albums, but he was not phased or concerned in the slightest. (The closest nervous-experience I'd had to this was when I handed my magazine to beloved visual artist and Destroy All Monsters member Mike Kelley with his art cannibalized in it—mercifully he said, "Just give me a copy." Done, whew). Brown had an ageless spark in his eyes I cannot define, but as the God of Hellfire, who had all but originated horror rock, glam, prog, psychedelic soul, even new wave (via early synthesizer/drum machine use), this was no surprise. Casually hearing that KISS stole the make-up idea from him (which he heard via the nefarious Kim Fowley), who his favorite Dr. Strange artist was (Colan over Ditko!), how his flaming helmet used to malfunction and burn his head, and the always-spiritual core of his music, was an absolute life-peak for me, and seemingly a manifestation of everything I ever held dear for my entire existence, crammed into but a few glorious hours.

Brown proclaimed in one of my favorite songs of all time, "Time Captives":

"We seek a void where creation once cried 'OM!' We synthesize the rays powering your brain-we are time captains, we write the astral records of history."

Perhaps, less headily but just as righteously, James Baldwin said,

"The place in which I'll fit will not exist until I make it."

I want think I made this place for myself, and I do indeed write the astral records of history.

To not entirely pat myself on the back here (in a book about me, natch), I titled the first chapter here, "Arbitrary Illumination," for a reason. It's a made-up phrase that often rings through me mind, because I'm not sure how much of one's life is made by design, or merely stumbling through it like Forrest Dump, or better yet, the recovering druggie in my fave head film, Chippaqua (he encounters Allen Ginsberg, the Fugs, Last Poets, and Moondog along the way, and I actually did walk into the wrong elevator backstage with Last Poets once).

A lot of this journey was luck indeed, ala being in the right/wrong place at the wrong/right time, but luckily I know no other way at this past-middle-age point.

So, onward and astral-upward it goes, to the void...

Where creation once cried OM to a mind shown.

ALSO OUT ON FAR WEST

SONNY VINCENT	Snake Pit Therapy
BRENT L. SMITH	Pipe Dreams on Pico
JOSEPH MATICK	The Baba Books
KURT EISENLOHR	Stab the Remote
KANSAS BOWLING	A Cuddly Toys Companion
KANSAS BOWLING & PARKER LOVE BOWLING	Prewritten Letters for Your Convenience
CRAIG DYER	Heavier Than a Death in the Family
PARKER LOVE BOWLING	Rhododendron, Rhododendron
JENNIFER ROBIN	You Only Bend Once with a Spoonful of Mercury
JOSEPH MATICK	Cherry Wagon
RICHARD CABUT	Disorderly Magic
NORMAN DOUGLAS	Love and the Fear of Love
ELIZABETH ELLEN	Estranged
JEFFREY WENGROFSKY	The Wolfboy of Rego Park
HAKON ADALSTEINSSON	Our Broken Land
A FAR WEST ANTHOLOGY	Pretty Obscure
LILY LADY	NDA
NIKOLA PEPERA	Lay Down & Get Lost
JACK SKELLEY	Myth Lab
PETER CROWLEY	Down at Max's

farwestpress.com

+1 (541) FAR-WEST

Milton Keynes UK
Ingram Content Group UK Ltd.
UKHW041058190824
447135UK00001B/1

9 798988 735465